The I

A Guide to Self-Healing with Energy

by Sergio Rijo

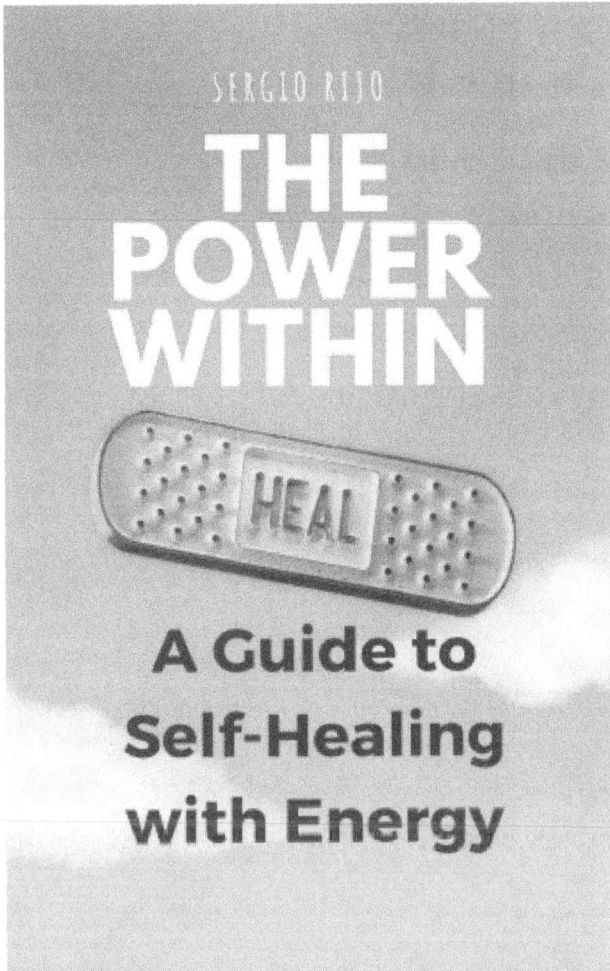

THE POWER WITHIN: A GUIDE TO SELF-HEALING WITH ENERGY

First edition. April 30, 2023.

Copyright © 2023 SERGIO RIJO.

ISBN: 979-8223327776

Written by SERGIO RIJO.

Table of Contents

Part 1:
Introduction

Chapter 1: What is Energy Healing?

The world we live in is full of energy. Everything around us is made up of energy, and it's constantly flowing and shifting. This energy affects us in many ways, from our thoughts and emotions to our physical bodies. Energy healing is the practice of using this energy to promote healing, balance, and wellness in our lives.

At its core, energy healing is based on the idea that our bodies have an energetic system that is just as important as our physical bodies. This system includes the chakras, meridians, and aura, which are all connected and work together to keep us healthy and balanced.

Energy healing techniques work by tapping into this energetic system and manipulating the energy flow to promote healing and balance. These techniques can range from simple practices like meditation and visualization to more complex modalities like Reiki and acupuncture.

One of the most important things to understand about energy healing is that it's not just about treating physical symptoms. In fact, energy healing is often used as a complementary therapy alongside traditional medical treatments. By addressing the root causes of illness and imbalance, energy healing can help to promote overall wellness and improve quality of life.

Energy healing is also an empowering practice, as it allows us to take control of our own health and well-being. By learning how to work with our energetic system, we can develop a deeper understanding of ourselves and our bodies, and take steps to promote healing and balance on a daily basis.

But energy healing is not just about healing physical ailments. It's also about healing emotional wounds and spiritual imbalances. By working with our energetic system, we can release negative emotions and thought patterns, and develop a greater sense of inner peace and connection.

There are many different types of energy healing techniques, each with its own unique approach and benefits. Some of the most popular include Reiki, acupuncture, and crystal healing. But regardless of the specific technique used, the goal of energy healing is always the same: to promote healing, balance, and wellness in our lives.

In the next chapter, we'll take a deeper dive into the science behind energy healing, and explore how it works to promote healing and balance in our bodies and minds.

Chapter 2: The Science Behind Energy Healing

Energy healing is often seen as a mystical, esoteric practice. But the truth is, there is a growing body of scientific research that supports the effectiveness of energy healing techniques.

At its core, energy healing is based on the concept that everything in the universe is made up of energy. This includes our bodies, our thoughts, and even the objects and spaces around us. When this energy becomes blocked or disrupted, it can lead to physical, emotional, and spiritual imbalances.

Energy healing techniques work by manipulating this energy flow to promote healing and balance. This can include practices like Reiki, acupuncture, and crystal healing, which all work by tapping into the body's energetic system to restore balance and promote healing.

While some may view energy healing as a purely spiritual or emotional practice, there is actually a growing body of scientific research that supports its effectiveness. Studies have shown that energy healing can have a positive impact on a range of physical and emotional conditions, from chronic pain to anxiety and depression.

One of the key ways that energy healing works is by promoting the body's natural healing processes. Our bodies have an innate ability to heal themselves, but sometimes this healing process can become blocked or disrupted. Energy healing techniques work by clearing these blockages and promoting the body's natural healing abilities.

For example, acupuncture has been shown to stimulate the release of endorphins, which are natural painkillers produced by the body. Reiki, on the other hand, has been shown to reduce stress and anxiety by promoting relaxation and a sense of calm.

In addition to promoting physical healing, energy healing can also have a profound impact on our emotional and spiritual well-being. By working with the body's energetic system, energy healing can help us release negative emotions and thought patterns, and develop a greater sense of inner peace and connection.

But how exactly does energy healing work on a scientific level? While the mechanisms are not yet fully understood, there are a few theories that have been proposed.

One theory is that energy healing works by influencing the body's electromagnetic field. Our bodies generate a weak electromagnetic field, which can be detected and measured using sensitive equipment. Energy healing techniques may work by influencing this field, which in turn can have an impact on the body's overall energy flow and balance.

Another theory is that energy healing works by stimulating the body's nervous system. This can include activating the parasympathetic nervous system, which is responsible for the "rest and digest" response that helps the body relax and recover.

Regardless of the specific mechanisms involved, the fact remains that energy healing has been shown to have a positive impact on a range of physical, emotional, and spiritual conditions. And as our understanding of the body's energetic system continues to evolve, it's likely that we will discover even more ways in which energy healing can promote healing and balance in our lives.

In the next chapter, we'll explore the benefits of energy healing in more detail, and look at some of the specific conditions and issues that can be addressed with these powerful techniques.

Chapter 3: The Benefits of Energy Healing

Energy healing has been practiced for centuries, and for good reason. The benefits of energy healing are vast, and can have a positive impact on every aspect of our lives - from physical health to emotional and spiritual well-being.

In this chapter, we'll explore some of the key benefits of energy healing, and how these techniques can help you to achieve greater health, happiness, and harmony in your life.

Physical Health Benefits

One of the most well-known benefits of energy healing is its ability to promote physical healing and well-being. Energy healing techniques like Reiki, acupuncture, and acupressure have all been shown to have a positive impact on a range of physical conditions, from chronic pain to digestive issues and more.

One of the ways in which energy healing promotes physical healing is by improving circulation and reducing inflammation in the body. Acupuncture, for example, works by stimulating the flow of energy or qi in the body, which can help to reduce pain and inflammation and promote healing.

In addition to reducing pain and inflammation, energy healing techniques can also help to boost the immune system, reduce stress, and promote overall physical health and vitality.

Emotional and Mental Health Benefits

Energy healing isn't just good for the body - it's also incredibly beneficial for the mind and emotions. Energy healing techniques can help to reduce stress and anxiety, improve mood, and promote a sense of calm and well-being.

One of the key ways in which energy healing works on the emotional and mental level is by promoting the release of negative emotions and thought patterns. These negative emotions and thought patterns can become stuck in the body's energy system, leading to physical and emotional imbalances.

By working with the body's energetic system, energy healing techniques can help to release these negative emotions and thought patterns, promoting a greater sense of inner peace and emotional well-being.

Spiritual Benefits

Finally, energy healing can also have profound spiritual benefits. By promoting a greater sense of connection with ourselves and the world around us, energy healing techniques can help us to tap into our inner wisdom and intuition, and develop a deeper understanding of our place in the world.

Energy healing can also help to promote a greater sense of connection with something greater than ourselves - whether that be a higher power, the universe, or simply the interconnectedness of all things.

By cultivating this sense of connection and spiritual awareness, energy healing can help us to live more fulfilling and purposeful lives, and to find greater meaning and joy in our daily experiences.

In addition to these key benefits, energy healing can also have a range of other positive effects, from improving sleep quality to promoting better relationships and more. The exact benefits will vary depending on the specific techniques and practices used, as well as the individual's unique needs and circumstances.

But one thing is clear - energy healing has the potential to transform our lives in powerful and profound ways. By tapping into the power within, we can unlock greater levels of health, happiness, and harmony, and cultivate a deeper sense of connection with ourselves, others, and the world around us.

Chapter 4: The Importance of Self-Healing

In our fast-paced and often stressful modern world, it's easy to lose sight of the importance of self-healing. We often push ourselves to the brink, sacrificing our health and well-being in the pursuit of success, achievement, or simply getting through the day.

But the truth is that self-healing is essential for our physical, emotional, and spiritual health. It's not a luxury or a nice-to-have - it's a fundamental aspect of our well-being that we ignore at our peril.

In this chapter, we'll explore the importance of self-healing, and why taking the time to nurture ourselves is so essential in today's world.

The Power of Self-Healing

At its core, self-healing is about taking responsibility for our own health and well-being. It's about recognizing that we have the power within us to heal ourselves, both physically and emotionally, and taking action to harness that power.

Self-healing is not about rejecting traditional medical care or ignoring the advice of healthcare professionals. Rather, it's about working in partnership with these professionals, and taking an active role in our own healing process.

When we take ownership of our health and well-being, we become empowered to make positive changes in our lives. We can take steps to reduce stress, improve our diet and exercise habits, and cultivate healthy relationships - all of which can have a profound impact on our physical and emotional health.

The Dangers of Ignoring Self-Healing

When we neglect self-healing, we put ourselves at risk of a range of negative consequences. Physical health issues like chronic pain, fatigue, and disease can all result from chronic stress, poor diet, and lack of exercise.

Emotionally, neglecting self-healing can lead to anxiety, depression, and other mental health issues. When we don't take the time to nurture ourselves emotionally, we can become disconnected from our inner selves, leading to feelings of emptiness, loneliness, and despair.

Spiritually, neglecting self-healing can lead to a sense of disconnection from something greater than ourselves. Without taking the time to connect with our inner wisdom and intuition, we may feel lost or adrift in the world, lacking a sense of purpose or direction.

Ultimately, neglecting self-healing can lead to a life that feels unfulfilling and out of balance. We may find ourselves constantly chasing external validation and success, while feeling empty and unfulfilled inside.

The Benefits of Prioritizing Self-Healing

On the other hand, when we prioritize self-healing, we unlock a range of positive benefits. Physically, we can experience improved health, reduced pain, and greater vitality.

Emotionally, prioritizing self-healing can lead to increased resilience, improved relationships, and a greater sense of inner peace and contentment.

Spiritually, prioritizing self-healing can lead to a greater sense of connection with something greater than ourselves, and a deeper understanding of our place in the world.

But perhaps the greatest benefit of self-healing is the sense of empowerment and self-awareness it can bring. When we take the time to nurture ourselves, we become more attuned to our own needs and desires, and better equipped to navigate life's challenges with grace and resilience.

Tips for Prioritizing Self-Healing

If you're ready to prioritize self-healing in your life, there are a range of techniques and practices you can use to get started. Here are just a few ideas to consider:

Practice mindfulness meditation or yoga to help reduce stress and promote inner peace.

Make time for regular exercise, whether that's going for a daily walk, practicing yoga, or hitting the gym.

Eat a healthy, balanced diet that's rich in whole foods and nutrients.

Get plenty of rest and prioritize good sleep habits.

Spend time in nature, whether that's taking a hike in the woods or simply sitting in a park.

Explore different forms of self-care, such as aromatherapy, massage, or energy healing practices like Reiki.

Engage in creative pursuits that bring you joy, whether that's painting, writing, or playing music.

Connect with loved ones and cultivate healthy, supportive relationships.

Remember, the key to self-healing is to prioritize your own well-being and take an active role in your own health. By making small changes to your daily routine and committing to a regular self-care practice, you can unlock the power of self-healing and live a more vibrant, fulfilling life.

Part 2:

Understanding the Energy Body

Chapter 5: The Energy Body - An Overview

In the world of energy healing, the concept of the energy body is central to understanding how our physical, emotional, and spiritual health are interconnected. The energy body is the unseen network of energy that flows through and around our physical body, and it's a key component of many traditional healing practices, including acupuncture, Reiki, and Qi Gong.

In this chapter, we'll explore the energy body in more detail, examining its components and functions, and how it can impact our overall health and well-being.

Understanding the Energy Body

The energy body is made up of several components, including chakras, meridians, and the aura. Each of these components plays a different role in regulating the flow of energy through our body.

Chakras are the energy centers located along the spine, and they are associated with different emotional and physical functions. There are seven primary chakras, each with its own color and symbol, and when these energy centers are in balance, our energy flows freely, and we experience a sense of overall health and well-being.

Meridians are the pathways that carry energy through the body, and they are the focus of traditional Chinese medicine and acupuncture. These pathways are believed to regulate the flow of energy, or Qi, through the body, and when Qi is blocked or stagnant, it can lead to physical or emotional pain or illness.

The aura is the electromagnetic field that surrounds the body, and it's thought to reflect our overall health and well-being. The aura can be seen by some people as a subtle light or color, and it can change based on our emotional state, physical health, or spiritual well-being.

How the Energy Body Impacts Our Health

The energy body is interconnected with our physical, emotional, and spiritual health, and imbalances in our energy can lead to a range of health issues.

For example, if the energy in our throat chakra is blocked, we may experience issues with communication, and we may struggle to express ourselves effectively. If the energy in our solar plexus chakra is imbalanced, we may struggle with self-esteem or confidence issues, and we may feel a sense of powerlessness or helplessness.

Similarly, if the energy flow through our meridians is blocked, we may experience physical pain or discomfort in specific parts of our body, or we may feel a sense of emotional heaviness or lethargy.

When we work to restore balance to our energy body, we can experience a sense of overall health and well-being. This can manifest in many ways, from improved physical health and reduced pain to increased emotional resilience and a greater sense of spiritual connection.

Tools for Balancing the Energy Body

There are a range of tools and techniques that can be used to balance the energy body, and these can vary depending on the individual's needs and preferences.

Some common tools for balancing the energy body include:

Meditation: Practicing mindfulness meditation can help us to become more aware of our energy body and to regulate our energy flow.

Reiki: Reiki is a Japanese healing technique that involves the transfer of energy through the practitioner's hands to the client's body.

Acupuncture: Acupuncture is a traditional Chinese medicine practice that involves the insertion of thin needles into specific points on the body to regulate energy flow.

Yoga: Practicing yoga can help to balance the energy body by promoting physical flexibility and strength, as well as mental and emotional calm.

Crystal healing: Certain crystals are believed to have specific energy properties, and they can be used to balance the energy body by placing them on specific parts of the body or carrying them with us.

These are just a few examples of the many tools and techniques that can be used to balance the energy body. The key is to find what works best for you and to be consistent in your practice.

In addition to these tools, there are also lifestyle changes that can support a healthy energy body. Eating a balanced and nutritious diet, getting regular exercise, and getting enough sleep are all important for overall health and can support a healthy energy body as well.

It's also important to pay attention to our emotional and spiritual needs. Practicing self-care, engaging in activities that bring us joy and fulfillment, and cultivating positive relationships can all contribute to a sense of overall well-being and balance in our energy body.

The Mystical and Spiritual Aspect of the Energy Body

While the concept of the energy body is rooted in traditional healing practices, it also has a mystical and spiritual aspect that is important to explore.

Many spiritual traditions believe in the existence of a subtle energy body or spiritual aura that is connected to our soul or spirit. This energy body is believed to be a bridge between our physical body and our higher consciousness, and it's seen as a key component of our spiritual development.

In some spiritual traditions, the energy body is believed to be a reflection of our karma or spiritual state, and balancing the energy body is seen as a way to achieve spiritual growth or enlightenment.

Mystical experiences, such as near-death experiences or visions, are often described as involving a profound sense of connection to this energy body or spiritual realm, and many spiritual seekers engage in practices such as meditation or prayer in order to deepen this connection and explore the mystical aspects of the energy body.

While the mystical and spiritual aspects of the energy body may not be as tangible or measurable as its physical components, they are no less important in understanding the full scope of its impact on our health and well-being.

The Emotional and Psychological Aspect of the Energy Body

In addition to its physical and spiritual aspects, the energy body also has an emotional and psychological component that is important to explore.

Many traditional healing practices recognize the interconnectedness of our emotions and our physical health, and the energy body is seen as a key component of this connection.

For example, if we experience chronic stress or emotional trauma, this can manifest as physical pain or illness in our body. This is because our emotional state can impact the flow of energy through our meridians and chakras, leading to imbalances that can affect our overall health.

In order to restore balance to the energy body and promote overall health and well-being, it's important to address both the physical and emotional components of our health. This may involve working with a therapist or counselor to address emotional trauma or stress, as well as engaging in practices such as meditation or yoga to support the flow of energy through the body.

The energy body is a complex and interconnected network of energy that plays a key role in our overall health and well-being. Understanding the components and functions of the energy body, as well as its impact on our physical, emotional, and spiritual health, can help us to better care for ourselves and promote overall health and well-being.

Whether we approach the energy body from a traditional healing perspective or explore its mystical and spiritual aspects, the key is to remain open and curious, and to be willing to explore the full scope of its impact on our lives. By doing so, we can tap into the transformative power of the energy body and experience a greater sense of connection, healing, and fulfillment in our lives.

Chapter 6: The Chakras - A Deep Dive

The chakras are the seven energy centers located along the spine that play a crucial role in regulating the flow of energy through our body. Each chakra is associated with a specific physical and emotional function, and when these energy centers are in balance, we experience a sense of overall health and well-being. In this chapter, we'll take a deep dive into each of the seven chakras, exploring their functions, associated emotions, and ways to balance them.

Root Chakra

The root chakra, also known as the Muladhara chakra, is located at the base of the spine and is associated with our sense of safety and security. This chakra is associated with the color red and is represented by a four-petaled lotus flower.

When the root chakra is in balance, we feel grounded and secure in our physical body, and we have a sense of stability and safety in our environment. However, when the root chakra is imbalanced, we may experience feelings of anxiety, fear, or insecurity.

To balance the root chakra, we can focus on grounding practices, such as spending time in nature, practicing yoga, or meditation. We can also incorporate grounding foods into our diet, such as root vegetables, and practice affirmations that reinforce our sense of safety and security.

Sacral Chakra

The sacral chakra, or Svadhisthana chakra, is located in the lower abdomen and is associated with our emotions and creativity. This chakra is represented by a six-petaled lotus flower and is associated with the color orange.

When the sacral chakra is balanced, we feel emotionally stable and creatively inspired. However, when this chakra is imbalanced, we may experience a lack of creative energy, difficulty in expressing our emotions, or a sense of disconnection from our sexuality.

To balance the sacral chakra, we can practice creative expression, such as painting, writing, or dancing. We can also practice yoga poses that stimulate the sacral area, such as hip-opening poses, and incorporate orange-colored foods into our diet, such as carrots and oranges.

Solar Plexus Chakra

The solar plexus chakra, or Manipura chakra, is located in the upper abdomen and is associated with our sense of personal power and self-esteem. This chakra is represented by a ten-petaled lotus flower and is associated with the color yellow.

When the solar plexus chakra is balanced, we feel confident and empowered, and we have a strong sense of self-worth. However, when this chakra is imbalanced, we may experience low self-esteem, feelings of powerlessness, or a lack of confidence.

To balance the solar plexus chakra, we can practice activities that boost our self-confidence, such as public speaking or taking on new challenges. We can also practice yoga poses that activate the solar plexus, such as boat pose, and incorporate yellow-colored foods into our diet, such as bananas and yellow peppers.

Heart Chakra

The heart chakra, or Anahata chakra, is located in the center of the chest and is associated with our ability to give and receive love. This chakra is represented by a twelve-petaled lotus flower and is associated with the color green.

When the heart chakra is balanced, we feel open and loving towards ourselves and others, and we have a deep sense of compassion and empathy. However, when this chakra is imbalanced, we may experience difficulty in forming meaningful relationships or feel closed off to love and connection.

To balance the heart chakra, we can practice activities that promote self-love and compassion, such as meditation or journaling. We can also practice yoga poses that open the chest, such as camel pose, and incorporate green-colored foods into our diet, such as leafy greens and avocado.

Throat Chakra

The throat chakra, or Vishuddha chakra, is located in the throat and is associated with our ability to communicate and express ourselves. This chakra is represented by a sixteen-petaled lotus flower and is associated with the color blue.

When the throat chakra is balanced, we are able to express ourselves clearly and confidently, and we have the ability to communicate our needs and desires effectively. However, when this chakra is imbalanced, we may experience difficulty in speaking up or expressing ourselves, or we may struggle with communication issues in our relationships.

To balance the throat chakra, we can practice activities that promote clear communication, such as public speaking or writing. We can also practice yoga poses that stimulate the throat area, such as shoulder stand, and incorporate blue-colored foods into our diet, such as blueberries and blue potatoes.

Third Eye Chakra

The third eye chakra, or Ajna chakra, is located in the center of the forehead and is associated with our intuition and inner wisdom. This chakra is represented by a two-petaled lotus flower and is associated with the color indigo.

When the third eye chakra is balanced, we have a deep sense of intuition and inner knowing, and we are able to make decisions with clarity and confidence. However, when this chakra is imbalanced, we may experience a lack of clarity or confusion, or we may struggle with decision-making.

To balance the third eye chakra, we can practice activities that promote inner awareness, such as meditation or mindfulness practices. We can also practice yoga poses that stimulate the third eye area, such as child's pose, and incorporate indigo-colored foods into our diet, such as blackberries and purple cabbage.

Crown Chakra

The crown chakra, or Sahasrara chakra, is located at the top of the head and is associated with our connection to the divine and our sense of spirituality. This chakra is represented by a thousand-petaled lotus flower and is associated with the color violet or white.

When the crown chakra is balanced, we have a deep sense of connection to the universe and a strong spiritual practice. However, when this chakra is imbalanced, we may experience a lack of purpose or direction, or feel disconnected from our spiritual path.

To balance the crown chakra, we can practice activities that promote spiritual connection, such as prayer or meditation. We can also practice yoga poses that stimulate the crown area, such as headstand, and incorporate violet or white-colored foods into our diet, such as grapes or coconut.

The chakras are a powerful tool for understanding and balancing our energy centers, and by incorporating practices that stimulate each chakra, we can experience a greater sense of overall health and well-being. By working with these energy centers, we can unlock our inner potential and connect with our deepest selves, leading to a more fulfilling and balanced life.

Chapter 7: The Meridians - The Energy Pathways

As we dive deeper into the world of energy medicine, we cannot overlook the importance of the meridians. The meridians are the pathways through which energy flows in the body, and they are an essential part of traditional Chinese medicine.

According to traditional Chinese medicine, the meridians are responsible for the proper functioning of the body's organs, tissues, and systems. When the energy flowing through the meridians is blocked or stagnant, it can lead to physical and emotional imbalances, which can manifest as pain, illness, or disease.

There are twelve primary meridians in the body, each associated with a specific organ system, as well as two additional meridians that are considered "extraordinary" and are not associated with a specific organ system. In this chapter, we will explore each of the primary meridians and their associated organs and systems.

The Lung Meridian

The lung meridian is the first meridian in the body and runs from the tip of the thumb to the upper chest. This meridian is associated with the lungs and the respiratory system and is responsible for the proper functioning of the immune system.

When the lung meridian is imbalanced, it can manifest as respiratory issues, such as asthma or allergies, as well as a weakened immune system. To balance the lung meridian, we can practice deep breathing exercises, spend time in nature, or practice yoga poses that focus on the chest, such as cobra or upward facing dog.

The Large Intestine Meridian

The large intestine meridian runs from the tip of the index finger to the nostril on the same side of the face. This meridian is associated with the large intestine and is responsible for the elimination of waste from the body.

When the large intestine meridian is imbalanced, it can manifest as digestive issues, such as constipation or diarrhea, as well as skin issues, such as acne or eczema. To balance the large intestine meridian, we can incorporate more fiber into our diet, drink plenty of water, and practice yoga poses that involve twisting, such as seated spinal twist.

The Stomach Meridian

The stomach meridian runs from the lower face to the second toe and is associated with the stomach and digestive system. This meridian is responsible for breaking down food and extracting nutrients from it.

When the stomach meridian is imbalanced, it can manifest as digestive issues, such as bloating or indigestion, as well as emotional imbalances, such as anxiety or worry. To balance the stomach meridian, we can practice mindful eating, chew our food thoroughly, and incorporate foods that are easy to digest, such as soups or stews, into our diet.

The Spleen Meridian

The spleen meridian runs from the big toe to the chest and is associated with the spleen and the immune system. This meridian is responsible for the proper functioning of the immune system and the distribution of nutrients throughout the body.

When the spleen meridian is imbalanced, it can manifest as weakened immunity, fatigue, or digestive issues, such as bloating or diarrhea. To balance the spleen meridian, we can incorporate foods that support the immune system, such as ginger or garlic, into our diet and practice yoga poses that focus on the abdomen, such as boat pose.

The Heart Meridian

The heart meridian runs from the armpit to the pinky finger and is associated with the heart and the circulatory system. This meridian is responsible for the proper flow of blood and oxygen throughout the body.

When the heart meridian is imbalanced, it can manifest as heart issues, such as high blood pressure or palpitations, as well as emotional imbalances, such as anxiety or depression. To balance the heart meridian, we can practice heart-opening yoga poses, such as camel or bridge pose, and focus on deep breathing exercises that expand the chest.

The Small Intestine Meridian

The small intestine meridian runs from the pinky finger to the ear and is associated with the small intestine and the digestive system. This meridian is responsible for the absorption of nutrients from food and the elimination of waste.

When the small intestine meridian is imbalanced, it can manifest as digestive issues, such as bloating or diarrhea, as well as emotional imbalances, such as indecisiveness or lack of clarity. To balance the small intestine meridian, we can incorporate foods that support gut health, such as fermented foods or probiotics, into our diet and practice yoga poses that involve twists, such as seated spinal twist or half lord of the fishes pose.

The Bladder Meridian

The bladder meridian runs from the inner corner of the eye to the pinky toe and is associated with the bladder and urinary system. This meridian is responsible for the elimination of waste from the body.

When the bladder meridian is imbalanced, it can manifest as urinary issues, such as incontinence or frequent urination, as well as emotional imbalances, such as fear or insecurity. To balance the bladder meridian, we can practice deep breathing exercises that focus on the lower abdomen and practice yoga poses that involve forward folds, such as seated forward bend or standing forward fold.

The Kidney Meridian

The kidney meridian runs from the sole of the foot to the chest and is associated with the kidneys and urinary system. This meridian is responsible for the filtration of waste and the regulation of fluids in the body.

When the kidney meridian is imbalanced, it can manifest as urinary issues, such as frequent urination or bladder infections, as well as emotional imbalances, such as fear or anxiety. To balance the kidney meridian, we can incorporate foods that support kidney health, such as kidney beans or sweet potatoes, into our diet and practice yoga poses that involve forward bends, such as standing forward fold or seated forward bend.

The Pericardium Meridian

The pericardium meridian runs from the chest to the middle finger and is associated with the heart and circulatory system. This meridian is responsible for the circulation of blood and the regulation of body temperature.

When the pericardium meridian is imbalanced, it can manifest as heart issues, such as palpitations or chest pain, as well as emotional imbalances, such as mood swings or lack of emotional connection. To balance the pericardium meridian, we can practice heart-opening yoga poses, such as camel or bridge pose, and practice mindfulness exercises that focus on emotional awareness.

The Triple Burner Meridian

The triple burner meridian runs from the outer corner of the eye to the fourth finger and is associated with the endocrine system and metabolism. This meridian is responsible for the regulation of hormones and the distribution of energy throughout the body.

When the triple burner meridian is imbalanced, it can manifest as hormonal imbalances, such as irregular periods or mood swings, as well as digestive issues, such as bloating or constipation. To balance the triple burner meridian, we can incorporate foods that support hormonal balance, such as leafy greens or omega-3 fatty acids, into our diet and practice yoga poses that involve twists, such as seated spinal twist or half lord of the fishes pose.

The Gallbladder Meridian

The gallbladder meridian runs from the outer corner of the eye to the fourth toe and is associated with the gallbladder and liver. This meridian is responsible for the detoxification of the body and the regulation of emotions.

When the gallbladder meridian is imbalanced, it can manifest as digestive issues, such as indigestion or nausea, as well as emotional imbalances, such as irritability or anger. To balance the gallbladder meridian, we can incorporate foods that support liver health, such as leafy greens and beets, into our diet and practice yoga poses that involve twists, such as seated spinal twist or twisted triangle pose. Additionally, practicing mindfulness exercises that focus on releasing anger and promoting forgiveness can also be helpful in balancing this meridian.

The Liver Meridian

The liver meridian runs from the big toe to the fourth finger and is associated with the liver and the proper flow of energy and blood throughout the body. This meridian is responsible for the detoxification of the body and the smooth flow of emotions.

When the liver meridian is imbalanced, it can manifest as digestive issues, such as indigestion or nausea, as well as emotional imbalances, such as irritability or anger. To balance the liver meridian, we can incorporate foods that support liver health, such as leafy greens and beets, into our diet and practice yoga poses that involve twists, such as seated spinal twist or twisted triangle pose. Additionally, practicing mindfulness exercises that focus on releasing anger and promoting forgiveness can also be helpful in balancing this meridian.

Chapter 8: The Aura: The Energy Field

The aura, also known as the energy field, is a fascinating and mysterious concept that has captured the attention of many people throughout the ages. It is said to be a field of energy that surrounds every living being, and it is believed to contain information about a person's physical, emotional, mental, and spiritual state. In this chapter, we will explore the aura, its significance, and how to work with it.

The aura is an invisible field of energy that surrounds every living being. It is composed of several layers, each with a different frequency and color. The aura is said to be a reflection of a person's physical, emotional, mental, and spiritual state, and it is believed to contain information about a person's past, present, and future.

One way to visualize the aura is to imagine it as a colorful egg-shaped field of energy that surrounds the body. This field extends several feet from the body and can be seen or sensed by people who have developed the ability to do so.

The colors of the aura are said to reflect a person's state of being. For example, red is associated with passion, courage, and vitality, while blue is associated with communication, clarity, and calmness. Green is associated with healing, growth, and balance, while yellow is associated with creativity, joy, and intellect.

The aura can be affected by many things, including emotions, thoughts, and the environment. For example, negative emotions such as fear, anger, and sadness can cause the aura to become cloudy or dark. Positive emotions such as love, joy, and peace, on the other hand, can cause the aura to become bright and vibrant.

The aura is also believed to be affected by the environment. For example, spending time in nature or near a body of water can help to cleanse and energize the aura, while spending time in a crowded, noisy, or polluted environment can have the opposite effect.

Working with the aura can be a powerful tool for personal growth and healing. There are many techniques that can be used to work with the aura, including meditation, visualization, and energy healing.

Meditation is a powerful tool for working with the aura. By focusing on the breath and quieting the mind, we can become more aware of our energy field and begin to sense its subtle nuances. Meditation can also help to clear the mind and release negative emotions, which can have a positive effect on the aura.

Visualization is another technique that can be used to work with the aura. By visualizing the aura as a bright, vibrant field of energy, we can begin to shift our energy and create a more positive state of being. Visualization can also be used to clear and balance the aura, as well as to protect it from negative influences.

Energy healing is a powerful technique for working with the aura. By using energy healing techniques such as Reiki or acupuncture, we can help to clear blockages in the aura and promote the free flow of energy throughout the body. Energy healing can also help to balance the chakras, which are energy centers located throughout the body that are believed to be connected to the aura.

In addition to these techniques, there are also many tools that can be used to work with the aura. Crystals, for example, are believed to have a powerful effect on the aura. By placing crystals on the body or wearing them as jewelry, we can help to balance and energize the aura.

Essential oils are another tool that can be used to work with the aura. By using essential oils such as lavender, frankincense, or rose, we can help to promote relaxation, balance, and harmony in the aura.

The aura is a fascinating and mysterious concept that has captured the attention of many people throughout the ages. It is believed to be a field of energy that surrounds every living being and contains information about a person's physical, emotional, mental, and spiritual state. The colors of the aura reflect a person's state of being and can be affected by emotions, thoughts, and the environment.

Working with the aura can be a powerful tool for personal growth and healing. Techniques such as meditation, visualization, and energy healing can be used to work with the aura, as well as tools such as crystals and essential oils.

One of the most important things to keep in mind when working with the aura is to approach it with an open mind and a sense of curiosity. It is easy to become skeptical or dismissive of something that we cannot see or touch, but the aura is a real and tangible field of energy that can be sensed and worked with.

Another important aspect of working with the aura is to be aware of our own energy and the impact that it has on others. When we are in a positive state of being, our aura can have a positive effect on those around us. On the other hand, when we are in a negative state of being, our aura can have a negative effect on those around us.

By working with the aura, we can learn to become more aware of our own energy and how it impacts our lives and the lives of those around us. We can also learn to become more in tune with our own physical, emotional, mental, and spiritual state, and work towards creating a more balanced and harmonious life.

In essence, the aura is a powerful tool for personal growth and healing. By working with it, we can learn to become more aware of our own energy and how it impacts our lives and the lives of those around us. We can also learn to become more in tune with our own physical, emotional, mental, and spiritual state, and work towards creating a more balanced and harmonious life.

Part 3:
Energy Healing Techniques

Chapter 9: Meditation for Energy Healing

Meditation is a powerful tool for promoting energy healing in the body. By quieting the mind and focusing on the breath, we can create a state of deep relaxation that allows the body to heal itself. In this chapter, we will explore the benefits of meditation for energy healing and discuss some techniques that can be used to incorporate meditation into your healing practice.

The Benefits of Meditation for Energy Healing

Meditation has been used for thousands of years to promote healing in the body, mind, and spirit. It is a powerful tool for reducing stress and promoting relaxation, which are essential for healing. When we are stressed, our body's natural healing processes are compromised, and we become more susceptible to illness and disease.

Meditation can help to reduce stress by calming the mind and promoting a state of deep relaxation. When we meditate, our brain waves slow down, and our body's natural healing processes are activated. Meditation has been shown to reduce the levels of stress hormones in the body, such as cortisol, which can have a negative impact on our health.

In addition to reducing stress, meditation can also help to boost our immune system, improve our mood, and promote a sense of overall well-being. Meditation has been shown to increase the production of antibodies in the body, which are essential for fighting off infection and disease. It has also been shown to increase the levels of neurotransmitters such as serotonin and dopamine, which are associated with feelings of happiness and well-being.

Meditation can also help to promote a sense of spiritual connection and inner peace. By connecting with our inner self, we can tap into a deeper sense of purpose and meaning in life. This can help to reduce feelings of anxiety, depression, and stress, which are often caused by a sense of disconnection from ourselves and others.

Techniques for Incorporating Meditation into Your Energy Healing Practice

There are many techniques that can be used to incorporate meditation into your energy healing practice. The following are some simple techniques that you can try:

Guided Meditation: Guided meditation is a great way to get started with meditation, especially if you are new to the practice. Guided meditation involves listening to a recording or a live teacher who guides you through the meditation process. This can be helpful for people who find it difficult to quiet their mind or who need extra support in their meditation practice.

Mantra Meditation: Mantra meditation involves repeating a word or phrase, such as "Om" or "Peace," over and over again. This can help to focus the mind and create a sense of inner calm. Mantra meditation is often used in conjunction with deep breathing exercises, which can help to further promote relaxation.

Body Scan Meditation: Body scan meditation involves focusing your attention on different parts of your body, one at a time, and noticing any sensations that you feel. This can help to bring awareness to areas of tension or discomfort in the body, and promote relaxation and healing.

Breath Awareness Meditation: Breath awareness meditation involves focusing your attention on your breath, noticing the sensation of the breath as it enters and leaves the body. This can help to calm the mind and promote relaxation.

Chakra Meditation: Chakra meditation involves focusing your attention on the seven energy centers of the body, known as chakras. By visualizing each chakra and focusing on its associated color and energy, we can help to balance and energize the body's energy system.

Tips for a Successful Meditation Practice

To get the most out of your meditation practice, it is important to create a comfortable and peaceful environment for yourself. Find a quiet space where you won't be disturbed, and create a relaxing atmosphere with candles, incense, or soft music.

It is also important to practice regularly, even if it is just for a few

minutes each day. Consistency is key when it comes to meditation, and the more you practice, the easier it will become to quiet your mind and focus on your breath.

Here are some additional tips for a successful meditation practice:

Set an intention: Before you begin your meditation practice, set an intention for what you hope to achieve. This could be anything from reducing stress and anxiety to promoting physical healing in the body. Having a clear intention can help to focus your mind and keep you motivated.

Start small: If you are new to meditation, start with just a few minutes each day and gradually increase the length of your sessions as you become more comfortable with the practice. It is better to meditate for a short amount of time consistently than to try and meditate for a long period of time sporadically.

Focus on your breath: Your breath is the foundation of your meditation practice, so it is important to focus on it throughout your session. Pay attention to the sensation of the breath as it enters and leaves your body, and try to let go of any distracting thoughts or feelings.

Be gentle with yourself: Meditation can be challenging, especially in the beginning. It is important to be gentle with yourself and not judge yourself harshly if you find your mind wandering or if you struggle to quiet your thoughts. Remember that meditation is a practice, and it takes time to develop the skills and techniques needed to meditate successfully.

Stay open-minded: Finally, it is important to approach your meditation practice with an open mind and a sense of curiosity. Meditation is a journey of self-discovery, and there is always more to learn and explore. Embrace the experience and stay open to new possibilities and insights.

Meditation is a powerful tool for promoting energy healing in the body. By quieting the mind and focusing on the breath, we can create a state of deep relaxation that allows the body to heal itself. Meditation has been shown to reduce stress, boost the immune system, improve mood, and promote a sense of spiritual connection and inner peace.

There are many techniques that can be used to incorporate meditation into your energy healing practice, including guided meditation, mantra meditation, body scan meditation, breath awareness meditation, and chakra meditation. By experimenting with different techniques and finding what works best for you, you can create a personalized meditation practice that supports your overall health and well-being.

Remember that meditation is a practice, and it takes time and dedication to develop the skills and techniques needed to meditate successfully. Be gentle with yourself, stay open-minded, and approach your meditation practice with a sense of curiosity and wonder. With patience and perseverance, you can harness the power of meditation to promote energy healing in your body, mind, and spirit.

Chapter 10: Visualization for Energy Healing

Visualization is a powerful tool for energy healing that can help to promote physical, emotional, and spiritual well-being. By using the power of our imagination, we can create a mental image of what we want to manifest in our lives, and this can help to bring about positive changes in our energy field.

In this chapter, we will explore the benefits of visualization for energy healing, discuss some techniques for incorporating visualization into your healing practice, and provide some tips for a successful visualization practice.

The Benefits of Visualization for Energy Healing

Visualization is a powerful tool for energy healing because it allows us to tap into the power of our subconscious mind. Our subconscious mind is responsible for our beliefs, emotions, and behaviors, and it plays a key role in our overall health and well-being.

When we visualize positive outcomes, we can create a shift in our subconscious mind, which can help to promote healing in our energy field. Visualization can also help to reduce stress and promote relaxation, which are essential for healing.

Research has shown that visualization can be an effective tool for reducing pain, anxiety, and depression. Visualization has also been shown to be effective in treating a variety of conditions, including cancer, asthma, and irritable bowel syndrome.

Techniques for Incorporating Visualization into Your Energy Healing Practice

There are many techniques that can be used to incorporate visualization into your energy healing practice. The following are some simple techniques that you can try:

Guided Visualization: Guided visualization involves listening to a recording or a live teacher who guides you through the visualization process. This can be helpful for people who find it difficult to create their own visualizations or who need extra support in their visualization practice.

Self-Guided Visualization: Self-guided visualization involves creating your own visualization and using your imagination to create a mental image of what you want to manifest in your life. This can be done in a quiet place where you won't be disturbed, and can be enhanced by using props such as candles or crystals.

Symbolic Visualization: Symbolic visualization involves using symbols or images to represent what you want to manifest in your life. For example, you might use a picture of a healthy body to represent your desire for physical healing, or a picture of a peaceful nature scene to represent your desire for emotional healing.

Energy Field Visualization: Energy field visualization involves visualizing your energy field as a bright, healthy, and vibrant energy field. You can use your imagination to visualize your energy field expanding and growing stronger, and you can also visualize any areas of your energy field that need healing or clearing.

Tips for a Successful Visualization Practice

To get the most out of your visualization practice, it is important to create a comfortable and peaceful environment for yourself. Find a quiet space where you won't be disturbed, and create a relaxing atmosphere with candles, incense, or soft music.

It is also important to be clear about what you want to manifest in your life. Spend some time thinking about what you want to achieve, and then create a mental image of what this looks like in your mind.

When you are visualizing, try to use all of your senses to create a vivid and realistic mental image. Use your imagination to create a picture in your mind, and then try to engage all of your senses by imagining what it would feel like, smell like, and sound like.

Finally, it is important to practice regularly. Set aside some time each day to practice visualization, and make it a part of your daily routine. The more you practice, the more effective your visualization practice will become.

Visualization is a powerful tool for energy healing that can help to promote physical, emotional, and spiritual well-being. By using the power of our imagination, we can create a mental image of what we want to manifest in our lives, and this can help to bring about positive changes in our energy field. Visualization can be incorporated into your energy healing practice in a variety of ways, including guided visualization, self-guided visualization, symbolic visualization, and energy field visualization.

To get the most out of your visualization practice, it is important to create a comfortable and peaceful environment for yourself, be clear about what you want to manifest in your life, engage all of your senses to create a vivid and realistic mental image, and practice regularly.

Visualization can be a powerful tool for promoting healing and well-being, but it is important to remember that it is not a substitute for medical or professional advice. If you are dealing with a serious health condition, it is important to seek the advice of a qualified healthcare provider.

Incorporating visualization into your energy healing practice can be a transformative experience, and can help you to tap into your own inner wisdom and intuition. By connecting with your inner self and the power of your subconscious mind, you can create positive changes in your life and promote healing and well-being on all levels.

Chapter 11: Breathing Techniques for Energy Healing

Breath is the essence of life, and it is also a powerful tool for energy healing. Breathing techniques have been used for thousands of years in various healing modalities to promote physical, emotional, and spiritual well-being. In this chapter, we will explore the benefits of breathing techniques for energy healing, discuss some of the most effective techniques, and provide tips for incorporating them into your healing practice.

The Benefits of Breathing Techniques for Energy Healing

Breathing techniques are a simple yet powerful way to promote energy flow throughout the body. When we breathe deeply and consciously, we can release tension and stress, improve circulation, and boost our immune system. Breathing techniques can also help to regulate the nervous system, calm the mind, and promote a sense of well-being.

Research has shown that breathing techniques can be an effective tool for reducing anxiety, depression, and chronic pain. They can also help to lower blood pressure, improve digestion, and promote better sleep. Breathing techniques are easy to learn and can be practiced anywhere, making them an accessible tool for anyone looking to improve their overall health and well-being.

Effective Breathing Techniques for Energy Healing

There are many different breathing techniques that can be used for energy healing. The following are some of the most effective techniques:

Abdominal Breathing: Also known as diaphragmatic breathing, this technique involves breathing deeply into the belly, allowing the diaphragm to expand and contract. This can help to reduce stress and promote relaxation.

To practice abdominal breathing, sit or lie down in a comfortable position. Place one hand on your belly and one hand on your chest. Take a deep breath in through your nose, allowing your belly to expand. Exhale slowly through your mouth, letting your belly deflate. Repeat for several breaths.

Alternate Nostril Breathing: This technique involves alternating between breathing through the left and right nostrils. It can help to balance the nervous system and promote a sense of calm.

To practice alternate nostril breathing, sit in a comfortable position and place your right thumb over your right nostril. Inhale deeply through your left nostril, then use your ring finger to close your left nostril and exhale through your right nostril. Inhale through your right nostril, then use your thumb to close your right nostril and exhale through your left nostril. Repeat for several rounds.

Breath of Fire: This is a powerful technique that involves rapid, rhythmic breathing through the nose. It can help to increase energy and promote mental clarity.

To practice Breath of Fire, sit in a comfortable position with your spine straight. Take a deep breath in through your nose, then exhale forcefully through your nose, pumping your belly rapidly. Continue this rhythmic breathing for several rounds.

Box Breathing: This technique involves breathing in a pattern of four counts in, four counts hold, four counts out, and four counts hold. It can help to promote relaxation and reduce stress.

To practice box breathing, sit in a comfortable position and inhale deeply through your nose for a count of four. Hold your breath for a count of four, then exhale slowly through your mouth for a count of four. Hold your breath for a count of four before inhaling again. Repeat for several rounds.

Tips for Incorporating Breathing Techniques into Your Healing Practice

To get the most out of your breathing practice, it is important to create a comfortable and peaceful environment for yourself. Find a quiet space where you won't be disturbed, and create a relaxing atmosphere with candles, incense, or soft music.

It is also important to be clear about your intentions for your breathing practice. Spend some time thinking about what you want to achieve, and set an intention for your practice. This could be something as simple as wanting to release stress, or something more specific, such as wanting to promote healing in a particular area of your body.

When practicing breathing techniques for energy healing, it is important to pay attention to your breath and your body. Focus on the sensation of the breath moving in and out of your body, and notice any areas of tension or discomfort. If you feel any discomfort or pain, adjust your breathing or posture accordingly.

It can also be helpful to incorporate visualization or affirmations into your breathing practice. For example, you could visualize healing energy flowing through your body with each inhale, and releasing tension and negativity with each exhale. Or, you could repeat a positive affirmation, such as "I am healthy and strong," with each breath.

Finally, be patient and consistent with your breathing practice. Like any form of energy healing, it takes time and dedication to see results. Set aside time each day for your practice, even if it's just a few minutes, and be gentle with yourself as you navigate any challenges or setbacks.

Breathing techniques are a powerful tool for energy healing that can promote physical, emotional, and spiritual well-being. By incorporating these techniques into your healing practice and being consistent and patient with your practice, you can experience the many benefits of conscious breathing for yourself. Remember, breath is the essence of life, and by harnessing its power, you can tap into a deeper sense of vitality and inner peace.

Chapter 12: Sound Therapy for Energy Healing

Sound therapy is a powerful and ancient healing practice that has been used for thousands of years in various cultures around the world. The use of sound for healing is based on the principle that everything in the universe is made up of energy and vibration, including our bodies. When we are healthy, our energy is in balance and flowing freely. However, when we are sick or out of balance, our energy becomes blocked, causing physical, emotional, and spiritual discomfort. Sound therapy works by using specific sounds and vibrations to help release these blockages and restore balance and harmony to the body, mind, and spirit.

In this chapter, we will explore the benefits of sound therapy for energy healing, discuss some of the most effective sound healing tools and techniques, and provide tips for incorporating sound therapy into your healing practice.

The Benefits of Sound Therapy for Energy Healing

Sound therapy can be a powerful tool for promoting energy flow throughout the body. When we listen to or produce certain sounds and vibrations, they can stimulate the cells in our body and promote healing. Sound therapy has been shown to be effective in reducing stress and anxiety, improving sleep, boosting the immune system, and promoting overall well-being.

Sound therapy can also be an effective tool for addressing specific health concerns. For example, specific frequencies and sounds can be used to target specific areas of the body, such as the lungs or the heart. Sound therapy can also be used to alleviate pain, reduce inflammation, and promote healing after surgery or injury.

Effective Sound Healing Tools and Techniques

There are many different sound healing tools and techniques that can be used for energy healing. The following are some of the most effective tools and techniques:

Tibetan Singing Bowls: These bowls are made of a special alloy of metals that produce a unique sound when struck or played. The bowls are often used in sound healing sessions to promote relaxation and reduce stress.

To use Tibetan singing bowls for energy healing, simply strike the bowl with a mallet and let the sound resonate throughout the room. Alternatively, you can play the bowl by running the mallet around the rim, creating a continuous and soothing sound.

Crystal Singing Bowls: These bowls are made of pure quartz crystal and produce a pure, clear tone when played. The bowls are often used in sound healing sessions to promote balance and harmony in the body.

To use crystal singing bowls for energy healing, simply strike the bowl with a mallet or play the bowl by running the mallet around the rim. The sound of the bowl will resonate throughout the room and promote healing and balance.

Tuning Forks: Tuning forks are metal instruments that produce a specific frequency when struck. They are often used in sound healing sessions to target specific areas of the body or to promote relaxation and balance.

To use tuning forks for energy healing, simply strike the fork and hold it near the area of the body you wish to target. The sound and vibrations of the fork will penetrate the body and promote healing.

Gongs: Gongs are large metal instruments that produce a deep, resonant sound when struck. They are often used in sound healing sessions to promote deep relaxation and reduce stress.

To use a gong for energy healing, simply strike the gong and let the sound resonate throughout the room. The sound of the gong will penetrate the body and promote deep relaxation and healing.

Tips for Incorporating Sound Therapy into Your Healing Practice

To get the most out of your sound healing practice, it is important to create a comfortable and peaceful environment for yourself. Find a quiet space where you won't be disturbed, and create a relaxing atmosphere with candles, incense, or soft lighting.

It is also important to be clear about your intentions for your sound healing practice. Spend some time thinking about what you want to achieve, and choose the appropriate tools and techniques to support your goals. If you are looking to promote relaxation and reduce stress, for example, you may want to use Tibetan singing bowls or gongs. If you are looking to target a specific area of the body, tuning forks may be the best choice.

When using sound therapy for energy healing, it is important to approach the practice with an open and receptive mindset. Allow yourself to fully immerse in the experience, and be open to the sounds and vibrations that are being produced. You may find that certain sounds or frequencies resonate with you more than others, and that is perfectly normal.

In addition to using sound healing tools and techniques, you may also want to incorporate chanting, singing, or playing musical instruments into your practice. These activities can help to further promote energy flow throughout the body and enhance the overall healing experience.

Finally, it is important to approach sound therapy for energy healing as a complementary practice, rather than a substitute for traditional medical care. While sound therapy can be a powerful tool for promoting healing, it should not be used as a replacement for medical treatment.

Sound therapy is a powerful and ancient healing practice that has been used for thousands of years to promote energy flow and restore balance and harmony to the body, mind, and spirit. By incorporating sound healing tools and techniques into your healing practice, you can reduce stress, improve sleep, boost the immune system, and promote overall well-being. So why not try incorporating sound therapy into your healing practice today and experience the power of sound for yourself?

Chapter 13: Crystal Healing for Energy Healing

Crystals have been revered for their beauty and mystical properties for thousands of years. In recent times, the use of crystals for healing has become increasingly popular. Crystal healing is based on the idea that crystals have their own unique energetic properties that can interact with the energies of our bodies, promoting healing and balance.

In this chapter, we will explore the benefits of crystal healing for energy healing, discuss some of the most effective crystal healing tools and techniques, and provide tips for incorporating crystal healing into your healing practice.

The Benefits of Crystal Healing for Energy Healing

Crystal healing is a powerful tool for promoting energy flow throughout the body. When we hold or place crystals on specific areas of the body, they can help to release blockages and promote healing. Crystal healing has been shown to be effective in reducing stress and anxiety, improving sleep, boosting the immune system, and promoting overall well-being.

Crystal healing can also be an effective tool for addressing specific health concerns. For example, specific crystals can be used to target specific areas of the body, such as the lungs or the heart. Crystals can also be used to alleviate pain, reduce inflammation, and promote healing after surgery or injury.

Effective Crystal Healing Tools and Techniques

There are many different crystal healing tools and techniques that can be used for energy healing. The following are some of the most effective tools and techniques:

Crystal Grids: A crystal grid is a pattern of crystals placed in a specific geometric pattern to amplify their energy and promote healing. To create a crystal grid, choose a pattern that resonates with your intentions, such as a flower of life or a sacred geometry symbol. Then, place the crystals in the pattern, focusing on your intentions and visualizing the energy flowing through the crystals.

Crystal Wands: A crystal wand is a pointed crystal that can be used to direct energy to specific areas of the body. To use a crystal wand, hold the pointed end to the area of the body you wish to target and visualize the energy flowing through the crystal and into your body.

Crystal Elixirs: A crystal elixir is a liquid that has been infused with the energetic properties of a crystal. To create a crystal elixir, simply place the crystal in a glass of water and let it sit for several hours. The water will absorb the energetic properties of the crystal, creating a powerful elixir that can be used for healing.

Crystal Meditation: Crystal meditation is a powerful tool for promoting relaxation and balance. To meditate with crystals, simply hold the crystal in your hand or place it on your body and focus on its energy. Visualize the energy flowing through your body, promoting healing and balance.

Tips for Incorporating Crystal Healing into Your Healing Practice

To get the most out of your crystal healing practice, it is important to choose the right crystals for your intentions. Spend some time researching the energetic properties of different crystals and choose the ones that resonate with your needs.

It is also important to cleanse and charge your crystals regularly. Crystals can absorb negative energy over time, which can affect their effectiveness. To cleanse your crystals, simply place them under running water or in a bowl of salt water for several hours. To charge your crystals, place them in the sun or moonlight for several hours.

When using crystals for healing, it is important to create a peaceful and relaxing environment for yourself. Find a quiet space where you won't be disturbed, and create a calming atmosphere with candles, incense, or soft lighting.

Crystal healing is a powerful and ancient practice that can be used to promote healing and balance in the body, mind, and spirit. By choosing the right crystals and using effective techniques, you can harness the power of crystals to promote energy flow and restore balance and harmony to your life.

Remember to approach crystal healing with an open mind and heart, allowing the energetic properties of the crystals to guide you towards healing and transformation. Trust in the power of the crystals and the innate wisdom of your body to promote healing and balance.

Crystal healing is a complementary therapy and should never be used as a replacement for traditional medical treatments. Always consult with your healthcare provider before using crystals or any other complementary therapies.

Incorporating crystal healing into your healing practice can be a beautiful and transformative experience. It is a powerful tool for promoting self-care, mindfulness, and spiritual growth. Whether you are new to crystal healing or an experienced practitioner, the benefits of this ancient practice are undeniable.

So, take some time to explore the world of crystal healing and discover the powerful healing properties of these beautiful and mystical gems. Allow them to guide you towards balance, harmony, and healing, and open yourself up to the transformative power of crystal healing.

Chapter 14: Reiki - The Healing Touch

Throughout human history, people have searched for ways to alleviate their suffering and find inner peace. One of the most popular methods for achieving these goals is Reiki. Reiki is a form of energy healing that originated in Japan in the early 20th century. It is based on the idea that there is a universal life force energy that flows through all living things, and that this energy can be channeled to promote healing and balance.

In this chapter, we will explore the history and philosophy of Reiki, discuss the benefits of Reiki for healing, and provide tips for incorporating Reiki into your healing practice.

The History and Philosophy of Reiki:

Reiki was developed by a Japanese monk named Mikao Usui in the early 20th century. Usui was a student of Buddhism, and he spent many years studying ancient texts and practicing meditation. One day, while meditating on a mountain, Usui had a vision of a powerful energy that could be used for healing. He spent the next several years developing a system for channeling this energy, which he called Reiki.

The word Reiki comes from two Japanese words: "rei," which means universal, and "ki," which means life force energy. According to Reiki philosophy, this universal life force energy flows through all living things, and when it is blocked or disrupted, we experience pain, illness, and emotional distress. Reiki practitioners believe that by channeling this energy, they can help to release blockages and promote healing.

The Benefits of Reiki for Healing:

Reiki is a gentle and non-invasive form of healing that can be used to promote physical, emotional, and spiritual well-being. It is particularly effective for reducing stress and anxiety, promoting relaxation, and alleviating pain.

Studies have shown that Reiki can be effective for a wide range of health concerns, including chronic pain, depression, anxiety, and insomnia. Reiki has also been shown to be effective in reducing the side effects of cancer treatment, such as fatigue and nausea.

One of the unique aspects of Reiki is that it can be used in combination with other healing modalities, such as massage therapy or acupuncture. Reiki can help to enhance the effects of these treatments, promoting deeper relaxation and healing.

Incorporating Reiki into Your Healing Practice:

If you are interested in incorporating Reiki into your healing practice, there are several things you can do to get started. The first step is to receive a Reiki attunement from a Reiki master. This attunement will help to open your energy channels and allow you to channel Reiki energy.

Once you have received your attunement, you can begin practicing Reiki on yourself and others. To practice Reiki, simply place your hands on or near the area of the body that needs healing and visualize the energy flowing through your hands and into the person's body. You can also use symbols or mantras to enhance the effects of your Reiki practice.

It is important to remember that Reiki is a form of energy healing, and as such, it is important to create a peaceful and relaxing environment for your practice. Find a quiet space where you won't be disturbed, and create a calming atmosphere with candles, incense, or soft lighting.

Reiki is a powerful and effective form of energy healing that can be used to promote physical, emotional, and spiritual well-being. By channeling universal life force energy, Reiki practitioners can help to release blockages and promote healing and balance in the body and mind.

If you are interested in incorporating Reiki into your healing practice, the first step is to receive a Reiki attunement from a Reiki master. From there, you can begin practicing Reiki on yourself and others, and explore the many benefits of this ancient healing practice.

In addition to its healing benefits, Reiki also offers a spiritual component that can help to promote inner peace and connection to the universe. Many Reiki practitioners describe feeling a deep sense of peace and tranquility during their Reiki sessions, and some even report spiritual experiences or connections to higher powers.

Ultimately, Reiki is a form of healing that can be beneficial for anyone, regardless of their beliefs or background. Whether you are struggling with physical pain, emotional distress, or simply seeking greater inner peace, Reiki offers a gentle and effective way to promote healing and balance in your life.

So if you are curious about Reiki, don't hesitate to explore this powerful and ancient healing practice. With the guidance of a Reiki master and a commitment to your own healing journey, you can experience the profound benefits of Reiki and discover a new level of well-being and connection to the world around you.

Part 4:
Healing the Mind

Chapter 15: The Connection Between Energy and Mind

The human mind is a powerful force, capable of shaping our thoughts, emotions, and experiences. But what many people may not realize is that our minds are intimately connected to our energy systems, and the way we think and feel can have a profound impact on our physical and emotional health.

In this chapter, we will explore the connection between energy and mind, and discuss the ways in which we can use this connection to improve our overall health and well-being.

The Energy System:

Before we can understand the connection between energy and mind, it is important to have a basic understanding of the energy system in the body. According to traditional Chinese medicine and other energy healing practices, the body is made up of a network of energy channels or meridians that flow throughout the body.

This energy, known as Qi or Chi, is the vital force that sustains all living things. When the energy flow in our body is balanced and harmonious, we experience good health, vitality, and emotional well-being. However, when there is a disruption or blockage in the flow of energy, we may experience physical or emotional symptoms such as pain, fatigue, anxiety, or depression.

The Mind-Body Connection:

The connection between energy and mind is rooted in the mind-body connection, the idea that our thoughts, emotions, and behaviors can have a direct impact on our physical health. Research has shown that the brain and nervous system are intimately connected to the energy system in the body, and that the mind and body are in constant communication with one another.

For example, when we experience stress, our bodies release a hormone called cortisol, which can lead to physical symptoms such as headaches, muscle tension, and digestive issues. Similarly, when we experience emotional pain or trauma, it can manifest in the body as physical pain or illness.

This connection between the mind and body is also reflected in our energy system. When we experience negative emotions or thoughts, it can disrupt the flow of energy in our body, leading to blockages or imbalances. Conversely, when we cultivate positive emotions such as love, compassion, and gratitude, it can enhance the flow of energy in our body, promoting healing and well-being.

Using Energy to Heal the Mind:

Given the close connection between energy and mind, it is no surprise that many energy healing modalities focus on improving mental health and emotional well-being. Reiki, for example, is a form of energy healing that can be used to promote relaxation, reduce stress and anxiety, and improve overall emotional balance.

Other energy healing practices such as acupuncture and acupressure also work to promote mental and emotional health by stimulating specific energy points in the body. By activating these points, it can help to release blockages or imbalances in the energy system, promoting healing and well-being.

In addition to energy healing modalities, there are also a number of other practices that can be used to improve mental and emotional health through the energy system. Meditation, for example, is a powerful tool for cultivating mindfulness and reducing stress, which can enhance the flow of energy in the body.

Breathwork is another technique that can be used to enhance the flow of energy in the body and promote relaxation. By focusing on the breath and consciously regulating our breathing, we can help to release tension and blockages in the energy system, promoting healing and well-being.

Chapter 16: Overcoming Negative Thoughts and Emotions

Negative thoughts and emotions can be a source of great pain and suffering for many people. They can drain your energy, lower your mood, and prevent you from enjoying life to the fullest. Whether you are dealing with anxiety, depression, or simply feeling overwhelmed by negative thoughts, it is possible to overcome these challenges and cultivate a more positive outlook on life.

In this chapter, we will explore the nature of negative thoughts and emotions, and provide practical tips and techniques for overcoming them.

Understanding Negative Thoughts and Emotions:

Negative thoughts and emotions can arise from a variety of sources. They may be triggered by external events, such as a job loss or a relationship breakup, or they may be a result of internal factors, such as negative self-talk or past traumas.

Regardless of their origin, negative thoughts and emotions can take a toll on your mental and physical health. They can cause you to feel stuck, hopeless, and overwhelmed, making it difficult to take positive steps forward in your life.

One of the key factors in overcoming negative thoughts and emotions is to understand their nature. Negative thoughts and emotions are not permanent, nor are they indicative of your true self. They are simply passing experiences that arise and fall away like clouds in the sky.

The problem arises when we identify with our negative thoughts and emotions, believing them to be an integral part of who we are. We may also engage in negative self-talk, which only reinforces our negative beliefs and feelings.

Overcoming Negative Thoughts and Emotions:

While it can be challenging to overcome negative thoughts and emotions, it is not impossible. Here are some tips and techniques that can help you cultivate a more positive outlook on life:

Mindfulness Meditation: Mindfulness meditation is a powerful tool for cultivating awareness of your thoughts and emotions. By focusing your attention on the present moment, you can learn to observe your thoughts and emotions without getting caught up in them. This can help you develop a more compassionate and accepting attitude towards yourself and your experiences.

Positive Affirmations: Positive affirmations are simple statements that you can repeat to yourself to cultivate a more positive mindset. For example, you might say, "I am worthy of love and happiness," or "I am capable of achieving my goals." By repeating these affirmations regularly, you can begin to shift your focus from negative to positive thoughts.

Gratitude Practice: Gratitude is a powerful antidote to negative thoughts and emotions. By focusing on the things in your life that you are grateful for, you can cultivate a sense of joy and abundance. You might try starting a gratitude journal, where you write down three things each day that you are grateful for.

Cognitive Behavioral Therapy (CBT): CBT is a form of therapy that focuses on identifying and changing negative thought patterns. By working with a therapist, you can learn to recognize and challenge negative thoughts and beliefs, and replace them with more positive and constructive ones.

Physical Activity: Regular physical activity can be a powerful way to boost your mood and reduce stress. Exercise releases endorphins, which are natural mood-boosters. Even a short walk or yoga session can help you feel more energized and positive.

Self-Care: Taking care of yourself is essential for overcoming negative thoughts and emotions. This can include things like getting enough sleep, eating a healthy diet, and spending time doing activities that bring you joy and relaxation.

Seek Support: Finally, don't be afraid to seek support from others. Talking to a trusted friend, family member, or therapist can help you gain perspective on your thoughts and emotions, and provide you with the encouragement and support you need to move forward.

Overcoming negative thoughts and emotions is not always easy, but it is possible with the right mindset and techniques. By understanding the nature of negative thoughts and emotions, cultivating mindfulness, practicing gratitude, engaging in physical activity, and seeking support from others, you can begin to shift your focus towards a more positive and fulfilling life.

Remember that negative thoughts and emotions are not a reflection of your true self, and that you have the power to change your mindset and habits. It may take time and effort, but the rewards of a more positive and joyful life are well worth it.

So, take a deep breath, and know that you are capable of overcoming negative thoughts and emotions. With patience, self-compassion, and a commitment to personal growth, you can create a life filled with love, joy, and inner peace.

Chapter 17: Cultivating Positive Thoughts and Emotions

Positive thoughts and emotions are essential for living a fulfilling and happy life. They can help you feel more energized, motivated, and connected to the world around you. However, cultivating positive thoughts and emotions is not always easy, especially when you are faced with challenges and setbacks in life. In this chapter, we will explore some practical tips and techniques for cultivating positive thoughts and emotions, and living a more joyful and fulfilling life.

The Power of Positive Thinking:

Positive thinking is a powerful tool for cultivating positive thoughts and emotions. When you focus your attention on positive thoughts and beliefs, you can shift your mindset from one of scarcity and negativity to one of abundance and positivity. This can help you feel more confident, motivated, and happy in your daily life.

Here are some practical tips for cultivating positive thinking:

Practice Gratitude: Gratitude is one of the most powerful tools for cultivating positive thinking. When you focus on the things in your life that you are grateful for, you can shift your attention from what is lacking to what you already have. You might try starting a gratitude journal, where you write down three things each day that you are grateful for.

Positive Affirmations: Positive affirmations are simple statements that you can repeat to yourself to cultivate a more positive mindset. For example, you might say, "I am capable of achieving my goals," or "I am worthy of love and happiness." By repeating these affirmations regularly, you can begin to shift your focus from negative to positive thoughts.

Surround Yourself with Positive People: The people you surround yourself with can have a significant impact on your mindset and mood. Try to spend time with people who are positive, supportive, and uplifting, and avoid those who bring you down or make you feel negative.

Focus on Solutions, Not Problems: When you encounter challenges in life, try to focus on solutions rather than problems. Instead of dwelling on what went wrong, think about what you can do to make things better. This can help you feel more empowered and in control of your life.

Cultivating Positive Emotions:

Positive emotions, such as joy, love, and contentment, can also have a significant impact on your mental and physical health. When you cultivate positive emotions, you can improve your mood, reduce stress, and feel more connected to others.

Here are some practical tips for cultivating positive emotions:

Engage in Activities You Enjoy: Doing things that you enjoy can help you feel more positive and fulfilled in life. Whether it's taking a walk in nature, practicing a hobby, or spending time with loved ones, make time for activities that bring you joy and happiness.

Practice Mindfulness: Mindfulness is a powerful tool for cultivating positive emotions. By focusing your attention on the present moment, you can learn to appreciate the small joys in life and cultivate a sense of contentment and peace. You might try practicing mindful breathing, where you focus on your breath and the sensations in your body.

Express Gratitude: Expressing gratitude to others can help you feel more connected and positive. Whether it's thanking a friend for their support or expressing gratitude to a coworker for their help, take time to acknowledge and appreciate the people in your life.

Practice Loving-Kindness Meditation: Loving-kindness meditation is a type of meditation that involves focusing on feelings of love, compassion, and kindness towards yourself and others. By cultivating these positive emotions, you can improve your mood and feel more connected to those around you.

Cultivating positive thoughts and emotions is not always easy, but it is essential for living a fulfilling and joyful life. By practicing gratitude, positive affirmations, and surrounding yourself with positive people, you can shift your mindset from one of negativity to one of abundance and positivity. Similarly, engaging in activities you enjoy, practicing mindfulness, expressing gratitude, and practicing loving-kindness meditation can help you cultivate positive emotions like joy, love, and contentment.

It's important to remember that cultivating positive thoughts and emotions is an ongoing process. It requires consistent effort and practice. It's also important to acknowledge that setbacks and challenges are a natural part of life, and it's okay to experience negative emotions from time to time. However, by cultivating a positive mindset and positive emotions, you can develop resilience and the ability to bounce back from setbacks with greater ease.

Remember, your thoughts and emotions are powerful forces that can shape your experiences and perceptions of the world around you. By cultivating positivity, you can transform your life and the lives of those around you. So take a moment to reflect on the tips and techniques we've discussed in this chapter, and begin cultivating positive thoughts and emotions in your daily life. You might be surprised at how much of a difference it can make.

Chapter 18: Mindfulness and Energy Healing

In this modern era, where stress, anxiety, and depression have become a part of our daily lives, it is essential to find ways to cope with these issues. Mindfulness and energy healing are two practices that have gained popularity in recent years for their potential to help individuals find inner peace, balance, and healing.

Mindfulness

Mindfulness is a practice that involves focusing your attention on the present moment, without judgment. By doing so, you can develop a sense of clarity and calm, and reduce stress and anxiety. Mindfulness is rooted in ancient Buddhist practices, but has been adapted for modern-day use in various settings, including healthcare, education, and workplaces.

Here are some practical tips for incorporating mindfulness into your daily life:

Start with small steps: Begin by incorporating small moments of mindfulness into your daily routine. This could be taking a few deep breaths before starting your day, or taking a few minutes to focus on your breath during a break at work.

Practice mindful breathing: Mindful breathing involves focusing your attention on your breath, and the sensations of your body as you inhale and exhale. This can help you feel more grounded and present in the moment.

Practice mindful eating: Mindful eating involves paying attention to the sensations of your body as you eat, and savoring each bite. This can help you develop a greater appreciation for food and a deeper connection to your body.

Practice gratitude: Practicing gratitude involves focusing on the things in your life that you are thankful for. This can help you shift your focus from negative to positive thoughts, and improve your overall sense of well-being.

Energy Healing:

Energy healing is a practice that involves working with the body's energy systems to promote healing and balance. This can involve a range of techniques, including Reiki, acupuncture, and acupressure. Energy healing is based on the idea that the body has an energy field, and that imbalances or blockages in this field can lead to physical, emotional, and spiritual issues.

Here are some practical tips for incorporating energy healing into your daily life:

Seek out a qualified practitioner: If you are interested in energy healing, it is essential to seek out a qualified practitioner who can guide you through the process. Look for someone who is trained and certified in the technique you are interested in.

Practice self-healing: There are also techniques you can practice on your own to promote energy healing. This could include meditation, visualization, or self-massage.

Take care of your body: Your physical health can also have an impact on your energy field. Eating a healthy diet, getting enough sleep, and exercising regularly can help keep your energy field balanced and healthy.

Practice grounding: Grounding involves connecting with the earth's energy to promote balance and stability. This could involve walking barefoot on grass or dirt, or practicing a grounding meditation.

Combining Mindfulness and Energy Healing:

Combining mindfulness and energy healing can be a powerful way to promote healing and balance in your life. By focusing your attention on the present moment and connecting with your body's energy field, you can develop a deeper sense of self-awareness and promote overall well-being.

Here are some practical tips for combining mindfulness and energy healing:

Practice mindful breathing with visualization: During mindful breathing, visualize yourself inhaling positive energy and exhaling negative energy. This can help you focus on the energy flow in your body and promote balance.

Practice mindfulness during energy healing sessions: During energy healing sessions, try to remain present and aware of the sensations in your body. This can help you deepen your connection to the energy field and promote healing.

Practice gratitude during energy healing sessions: Take time to express gratitude to your practitioner and yourself for taking steps towards healing and balance. This can help cultivate a positive mindset and support your overall well-being.

Practice self care: Practicing self-care, such as taking time to rest, exercise, and nourish your body with healthy food, can support your energy field and overall health. Incorporating mindfulness practices into your self-care routine can also promote relaxation and reduce stress.

Incorporate mindfulness and energy healing into your daily routine: Incorporating mindfulness and energy healing practices into your daily routine can help you maintain a sense of balance and well-being. Whether it's taking a few deep breaths before starting your day or practicing a grounding meditation before bed, find ways to incorporate these practices into your daily routine.

Remember to be patient and kind to yourself as you embark on your mindfulness and energy healing journey. Healing and transformation take time, and it's important to approach these practices with an open and compassionate mindset. By incorporating mindfulness and energy healing into your life, you can cultivate a deeper sense of self-awareness, promote healing, and find inner peace and balance.

Part 5:
Healing the Body

Chapter 19: The Connection Between Energy and Body

The human body is a complex and magnificent creation, full of energy and life force. Every cell in our body is alive with energy, constantly moving and vibrating to maintain our health and vitality. The connection between energy and the body is an ancient concept that has been recognized by healers and mystics throughout history. In this chapter, we will explore the relationship between energy and the body, and how understanding this connection can enhance our physical, emotional, and spiritual well-being.

The Human Energy System:

The human body is composed of several energy systems that work together to create a harmonious flow of energy throughout the body. These systems include:

Chakras: Chakras are energy centers that run along the spine, from the base to the crown of the head. There are seven main chakras, each with its own unique energy and function.

Meridians: Meridians are energy pathways that run throughout the body. They are channels that transport energy to different parts of the body.

Aura: The aura is an energy field that surrounds the body. It is composed of several layers, each with its own unique energy and function.

The Flow of Energy in the Body:

The flow of energy in the body is essential for maintaining good health and well-being. When the energy in the body is flowing smoothly, we feel balanced and in harmony. When the energy is blocked or stagnant, we may experience physical, emotional, or spiritual issues.

Energy blockages can occur for various reasons, including stress, trauma, and illness. When energy is blocked, it can cause pain, discomfort, and disease. By understanding the flow of energy in the body, we can learn to recognize energy blockages and work to release them.

Here are some practical tips for enhancing the flow of energy in the body:

Practice Yoga: Yoga is an excellent way to enhance the flow of energy in the body. It combines physical postures, breathing exercises, and meditation to promote balance and harmony.

Receive Energy Healing: Energy healing is a practice that works with the body's energy systems to promote healing and balance. It can include techniques such as Reiki, acupuncture, and acupressure.

Practice Meditation: Meditation is a powerful tool for enhancing the flow of energy in the body. It promotes relaxation, reduces stress, and promotes mental clarity.

Eat a Healthy Diet: A healthy diet can also enhance the flow of energy in the body. Eating a diet rich in fruits, vegetables, and whole grains can provide the body with the nutrients it needs to function at its best.

The Connection Between Emotions and Energy:

Our emotions are also closely connected to the flow of energy in the body. When we experience emotions such as anger, fear, or sadness, it can cause energy blockages in the body. These blockages can lead to physical symptoms such as headaches, digestive issues, or muscle tension.

On the other hand, positive emotions such as love, joy, and gratitude can enhance the flow of energy in the body. When we experience these emotions, it can create a sense of well-being and promote good health.

Here are some practical tips for enhancing positive emotions and promoting the flow of energy in the body:

Practice Gratitude: Practicing gratitude can enhance positive emotions and promote the flow of energy in the body. Take time each day to reflect on the things in your life that you are thankful for.

Surround Yourself with Positive Energy: Surrounding yourself with positive energy can also enhance positive emotions and promote the flow of energy in the body. Spend time with people who uplift and inspire you.

Practice Self-Care: Taking care of yourself can also enhance positive emotions and promote the flow of energy in the body. This could include taking a relaxing bath, getting a massage, or spending time in nature.

Release Negative Emotions: It's also important to release negative emotions such as anger, fear, and sadness. One way to do this is through journaling or talking with a therapist. It's important to acknowledge and process these emotions to release any energy blockages they may be causing.

The Spiritual Connection:

The connection between energy and the body also extends to our spiritual well-being. Many spiritual practices focus on the flow of energy in the body and aim to enhance it for greater spiritual connection and growth.

Here are some spiritual practices that can enhance the flow of energy in the body:

Meditation: Meditation is a powerful tool for spiritual growth and enhancing the flow of energy in the body. It can help us connect with our inner selves and higher power.

Prayer: Prayer is another spiritual practice that can enhance the flow of energy in the body. It can help us connect with our higher power and promote feelings of peace and serenity.

Energy Healing: Energy healing can also be a powerful tool for spiritual growth. It can help us release any energy blockages that may be hindering our spiritual connection.

Visualization: Visualization is a technique that involves creating mental images to promote healing and well-being. It can be a powerful tool for enhancing the flow of energy in the body and promoting spiritual growth.

The connection between energy and the body is a complex and intricate concept that has been recognized for centuries. Understanding this connection and working to enhance the flow of energy in the body can lead to greater physical, emotional, and spiritual well-being.

By practicing yoga, receiving energy healing, meditating, eating a healthy diet, and releasing negative emotions, we can promote the flow of energy in the body and experience greater vitality and balance. Additionally, spiritual practices such as prayer, energy healing, and visualization can enhance our spiritual connection and promote growth.

The human body is a remarkable creation full of energy and life force. By nurturing and enhancing this energy, we can experience greater health, happiness, and well-being.

Chapter 20: Using Energy Healing for Pain Management

Pain is a common experience that we all go through at some point in our lives. Whether it's physical, emotional, or spiritual, pain can be a challenging and overwhelming experience. Fortunately, there are many ways to manage pain, and one of them is through energy healing.

Energy healing is a practice that works with the body's energy systems to promote healing and balance. It can include techniques such as Reiki, acupuncture, and acupressure. By using energy healing techniques, we can help to release blockages and promote the flow of energy in the body, which can help to alleviate pain.

In this chapter, we will explore the connection between energy healing and pain management and how you can use energy healing techniques to manage your pain.

Understanding Pain:

Pain is a complex experience that involves both physical and emotional components. It is a sensation that tells us something is wrong and needs attention. Pain can be acute, which means it is a sudden and intense sensation, or chronic, which means it is ongoing and persistent.

Physical pain can be caused by injury, illness, or disease, while emotional pain can be caused by stress, anxiety, or depression. Spiritual pain can be caused by a lack of meaning or purpose in life.

Managing Pain with Energy Healing:

Energy healing can be a useful tool for managing pain, whether it's physical, emotional, or spiritual. By working with the body's energy systems, energy healing can help to promote healing, release blockages, and restore balance.

Here are some energy healing techniques you can use for pain management:

Reiki: Reiki is a form of energy healing that involves the practitioner placing their hands on or near the body to promote healing and relaxation. It can be used to alleviate physical pain, emotional pain, and spiritual pain.

Acupuncture: Acupuncture is a technique that involves the insertion of thin needles into the skin to stimulate specific points on the body. It can be used to alleviate physical pain, emotional pain, and spiritual pain.

Acupressure: Acupressure is a technique that involves applying pressure to specific points on the body to promote healing and relaxation. It can be used to alleviate physical pain, emotional pain, and spiritual pain.

Meditation: Meditation is a powerful tool for managing pain. It promotes relaxation, reduces stress, and promotes mental clarity. By practicing meditation regularly, you can help to alleviate physical pain, emotional pain, and spiritual pain.

Breathing Exercises: Breathing exercises can also be helpful for managing pain. By focusing on your breath, you can promote relaxation and reduce stress, which can help to alleviate pain.

Visualization: Visualization is a technique that involves creating mental images to promote healing and relaxation. By visualizing yourself in a peaceful and healing environment, you can help to alleviate physical pain, emotional pain, and spiritual pain.

Combining Energy Healing Techniques:

Combining energy healing techniques can be an effective way to manage pain. For example, you could combine Reiki with meditation and visualization to create a powerful pain management practice. Or, you could combine acupuncture with breathing exercises to promote relaxation and reduce stress.

The key is to find the combination of energy healing techniques that works best for you and your unique needs. Experiment with different techniques and see which ones resonate with you the most.

The Benefits of Energy Healing for Pain Management:

There are many benefits to using energy healing for pain management. Here are some of the most significant benefits:

Natural: Energy healing is a natural approach to pain management. It doesn't involve medication or invasive procedures, which can be a significant benefit for those who prefer a more natural approach to healing.

Non-Invasive: Energy healing techniques are non-invasive, which means they don't require any incisions or injections. This can be a significant benefit for those who are afraid of needles or invasive procedures.

Holistic: Energy healing takes a holistic approach to healing, addressing not just the physical symptoms of pain but also the emotional and spiritual components. By addressing all aspects of pain, energy healing can provide a more comprehensive approach to pain management.

Personalized: Energy healing techniques can be customized to meet the unique needs of each individual. This personalized approach can be a significant benefit for those who have not found success with traditional pain management methods.

Side-Effect Free: Energy healing techniques are generally considered to be safe and have few side effects. This can be a significant benefit for those who are concerned about the side effects of medication or other traditional pain management methods.

Promotes Relaxation: Many energy healing techniques promote relaxation, which can be helpful for managing pain. By promoting relaxation, energy healing can help to reduce stress and promote a sense of calm, which can help to alleviate pain.

Promotes Self-Healing: Energy healing works with the body's natural healing processes, promoting self-healing. By promoting self-healing, energy healing can help to address the root causes of pain and promote long-term healing.

Tips for Using Energy Healing for Pain Management:

If you are interested in using energy healing for pain management, here are some tips to help you get started:

Find a qualified practitioner: If you are new to energy healing, it's a good idea to work with a qualified practitioner. Look for someone who is trained and experienced in the specific energy healing technique you are interested in.

Experiment with different techniques: There are many different energy healing techniques to choose from. Experiment with different techniques to find the ones that work best for you.

Be patient: Energy healing is not a quick fix. It takes time and patience to see results. Be patient and consistent with your practice.

Practice regularly: To see the best results, it's important to practice energy healing regularly. Set aside time each day to practice your chosen technique.

Be open-minded: Energy healing can be a new and unfamiliar experience for some people. Approach it with an open mind and be willing to try new things.

Pain is a challenging experience that can be overwhelming at times. Fortunately, there are many ways to manage pain, including energy healing. Energy healing works with the body's energy systems to promote healing and balance, which can help to alleviate pain.

There are many different energy healing techniques to choose from, including Reiki, acupuncture, and acupressure. By combining different techniques and customizing your approach, you can find the best approach for managing your pain.

Energy healing is a natural, non-invasive, and holistic approach to pain management. It promotes relaxation, self-healing, and has few side effects. If you are interested in using energy healing for pain management, find a qualified practitioner, experiment with different techniques, be patient, practice regularly, and approach it with an open mind. With the right approach, energy healing can be a powerful tool for managing pain and promoting healing.

Chapter 21: Your Immune System with Energy Healing

The immune system is a complex network of cells, tissues, and organs that work together to protect our bodies from harmful invaders such as viruses, bacteria, and parasites. It is our body's defense mechanism, and it is constantly working to keep us healthy and free from disease. However, sometimes our immune system can become weakened, making us more susceptible to illness and disease. That's where energy healing comes in.

Energy healing is a holistic approach to healing that focuses on the body's energy systems. It involves using various techniques to balance the body's energy, release blockages, and promote healing. Energy healing can be used to support and strengthen the immune system, helping to keep us healthy and free from disease.

Understanding the Immune System:

To understand how energy healing can support the immune system, we need to understand how the immune system works.

The immune system is made up of a variety of cells, tissues, and organs. These include:

White blood cells: These are the cells that fight off infection and disease. They identify and destroy harmful invaders in the body.

Lymphatic system: This is a network of vessels and tissues that helps to circulate lymph (a fluid that contains white blood cells) throughout the body.

Bone marrow: This is the spongy tissue inside our bones that produces red blood cells, white blood cells, and platelets.

Spleen: This is an organ located in the abdomen that helps to filter blood and remove old or damaged cells.

When our body is invaded by harmful pathogens, our immune system kicks into action. It sends white blood cells to attack and destroy the invaders. This can result in inflammation, which is our body's natural response to infection and injury. Inflammation can cause redness, swelling, and pain.

When our immune system is working correctly, it can quickly identify and destroy harmful invaders, keeping us healthy and free from disease. However, when our immune system is weakened, it may not be able to fight off infection and disease effectively.

Strengthening the Immune System with Energy Healing:

Energy healing can be used to support and strengthen the immune system. Here are some energy healing techniques you can use to support your immune system:

Reiki: Reiki is a form of energy healing that involves the practitioner placing their hands on or near the body to promote healing and relaxation. It can be used to support the immune system by promoting relaxation, reducing stress, and restoring balance to the body's energy systems.

Chakra balancing: The chakras are energy centers in the body that play a vital role in our health and well-being. Each chakra is associated with different organs and systems in the body. By balancing the chakras, we can promote overall health and well-being, including the health of the immune system.

Meditation: Meditation is a powerful tool for promoting relaxation and reducing stress. When we are stressed, our immune system can become weakened, making us more susceptible to illness and disease.

By practicing meditation regularly, we can help to reduce stress and support the immune system.

Visualization: Visualization is a technique that involves creating mental images to promote healing and relaxation. By visualizing yourself as healthy and vibrant, you can help to support your immune system and promote overall health and well-being.

Sound therapy: Sound therapy involves using sound vibrations to promote healing and relaxation. It can be used to support the immune system by reducing stress and promoting relaxation.

Crystal healing: Crystals are powerful tools for healing and promoting balance in the body's energy systems. They can be used to support the immune system by promoting overall health and well-being.

Combining Energy Healing Techniques:

Combining energy healing techniques can be an effective way to support and strengthen the immune system. For example, you could combine Reiki with chakra balancing and visualization for a powerful immune-boosting practice.

To begin, find a quiet and comfortable space where you won't be disturbed. Sit or lie down in a comfortable position and take a few deep breaths to center yourself.

Next, begin your Reiki practice by placing your hands on or near your body. Allow the energy to flow through your hands and into your body, promoting relaxation and restoring balance to your energy systems.

Once you feel relaxed and centered, move on to chakra balancing. Focus on each chakra, starting with the root chakra and working your way up to the crown chakra. Visualize each chakra as a spinning wheel of energy, and imagine each one becoming balanced and harmonious.

As you work on each chakra, you can also visualize yourself as healthy and vibrant, with a strong and resilient immune system. See yourself surrounded by a protective bubble of light, keeping harmful pathogens at bay.

Finally, end your practice with a visualization exercise. Imagine yourself as healthy and strong, with a radiant glow of energy surrounding you. See yourself going about your day, feeling confident and energized, with a powerful immune system protecting you from harm.

By combining these energy healing techniques, you can support and strengthen your immune system, promoting overall health and well-being.

The immune system is a vital part of our body's defense mechanism, protecting us from harmful invaders and keeping us healthy and free from disease. When our immune system is weakened, we may become more susceptible to illness and disease.

Energy healing is a powerful tool for supporting and strengthening the immune system. By using various techniques such as Reiki, chakra balancing, meditation, visualization, sound therapy, and crystal healing, we can promote relaxation, reduce stress, and restore balance to the body's energy systems.

By incorporating these energy healing practices into our daily lives, we can support our immune system and promote overall health and well-being. So take some time for yourself today, and give your immune system the support it needs to keep you healthy and thriving.

Chapter 22: Healing from Chronic Illness with Energy Healing

Chronic illness is a condition that lasts for an extended period of time, often for a person's entire life. Chronic illnesses can be caused by a variety of factors, such as genetics, lifestyle choices, or environmental factors. These conditions can be challenging to manage, and they can significantly impact a person's quality of life. However, energy healing can be a powerful tool for managing chronic illness and promoting healing.

Understanding Chronic Illness:

Chronic illness is a broad term that encompasses a range of conditions. Some common chronic illnesses include:

Diabetes

Arthritis

Asthma

Heart disease

Chronic obstructive pulmonary disease (COPD)

Chronic fatigue syndrome

Fibromyalgia

Multiple sclerosis

Cancer

These conditions can be debilitating and can significantly impact a person's quality of life. They often require ongoing treatment and management to prevent further complications.

Managing Chronic Illness with Energy Healing:

Energy healing can be a powerful tool for managing chronic illness. Here are some ways that energy healing can be used to promote healing and manage chronic illness:

Promoting relaxation: Chronic illness can be stressful and can cause anxiety and tension. Energy healing techniques, such as Reiki and meditation, can be used to promote relaxation and reduce stress.

Balancing energy: Chronic illness can disrupt the body's energy systems, causing blockages and imbalances. Energy healing techniques, such as chakra balancing and crystal healing, can be used to restore balance to the body's energy systems.

Reducing pain: Chronic illness can cause chronic pain, which can be challenging to manage. Energy healing techniques, such as sound therapy and acupuncture, can be used to reduce pain and promote healing.

Boosting the immune system: Chronic illness can weaken the immune system, making a person more susceptible to illness and infection. Energy healing techniques, such as Reiki and visualization, can be used to support the immune system and promote healing.

Reducing inflammation: Chronic illness can cause chronic inflammation, which can contribute to further complications. Energy healing techniques, such as sound therapy and meditation, can be used to reduce inflammation and promote healing.

Combining Energy Healing Techniques:

Combining energy healing techniques can be an effective way to manage chronic illness. For example, you could combine Reiki with chakra balancing and meditation to promote relaxation, restore balance to the body's energy systems, and reduce stress. Or you could combine sound therapy with crystal healing to reduce pain and inflammation and promote healing.

Energy Healing and Traditional Medicine:

It's essential to note that energy healing should not be used as a substitute for traditional medical treatment. Instead, it should be used as a complementary therapy to support traditional medical treatment. If you have a chronic illness, it's crucial to work with your healthcare provider to develop a treatment plan that includes both traditional medical treatment and energy healing.

It's also important to note that energy healing may not work for everyone. Every person's body is unique, and what works for one person may not work for another. However, many people have found that energy healing has been helpful in managing chronic illness and promoting healing.

The Role of Mindset:

One of the essential aspects of managing chronic illness with energy healing is mindset. A positive mindset can be a powerful tool for promoting healing and managing chronic illness. Here are some ways that mindset can impact healing:

Belief in healing: Belief in healing is a powerful tool for promoting healing. If you believe that you can heal, you are more likely to take actions that support healing, such as practicing energy healing techniques, eating a healthy diet, and getting regular exercise.

Positive attitude: A positive attitude can help you to manage the challenges of chronic illness. It can help you to stay motivated and focused on your healing journey, even when faced with setbacks or obstacles.

Visualization: Visualization is a powerful tool that can be used to support healing. By visualizing yourself as healthy and whole, you can help to create a positive mindset and promote healing.

Gratitude: Practicing gratitude can help you to stay positive and focused on the good in your life, even when dealing with the challenges of chronic illness.

Self-care: Self-care is an essential part of managing chronic illness. By taking care of yourself and practicing self-compassion, you can help to promote healing and manage the stress of living with a chronic illness.

Living with a chronic illness can be challenging, but energy healing can be a powerful tool for managing symptoms, promoting healing, and improving quality of life. By combining energy healing techniques with traditional medical treatment and adopting a positive mindset, you can take control of your health and manage your chronic illness in a way that works for you.

Remember, healing is a journey, and there may be setbacks along the way. But by staying focused on your goals, practicing self-care, and seeking support from healthcare providers, friends, and family, you can make progress towards healing and living a fulfilling life despite your chronic illness.

So, take the time to explore energy healing techniques and find what works for you. Whether it's Reiki, crystal healing, sound therapy, or another technique, know that you have the power to promote healing and manage your chronic illness.

Chapter 23: Energy Healing for Weight Management

Weight management can be a challenging journey for many people. It can be difficult to maintain a healthy weight, and there are many factors that can contribute to weight gain, including genetics, lifestyle choices, and environmental factors. However, energy healing can be a powerful tool for weight management. In this chapter, we will explore the ways that energy healing can be used to promote weight loss, improve body image, and support overall health and wellness.

Understanding Weight Management:

Weight management is the process of maintaining a healthy weight. A healthy weight is important for overall health and wellness, and it can help to prevent chronic diseases such as diabetes, heart disease, and cancer. However, maintaining a healthy weight can be challenging. Many factors can contribute to weight gain, including:

Unhealthy diet

Lack of exercise

Stress

Sleep deprivation

Genetics

Environmental factors

Managing Weight with Energy Healing:

Energy healing can be a powerful tool for weight management. Here are some ways that energy healing can be used to promote weight loss, improve body image, and support overall health and wellness.

Chakra Balancing:

Chakra balancing is a form of energy healing that can help to restore balance to the body's energy systems. The chakras are energy centers located throughout the body, and they are associated with different aspects of physical, emotional, and spiritual health. When the chakras are balanced, energy can flow freely throughout the body, promoting health and wellness.

Chakra balancing can be used to support weight management by addressing the underlying emotional and spiritual factors that may contribute to weight gain. For example, the root chakra, located at the base of the spine, is associated with issues of survival and security. If this chakra is blocked, it can contribute to feelings of insecurity and anxiety, which may lead to overeating as a coping mechanism. By balancing the root chakra, it may be possible to reduce feelings of anxiety and improve overall emotional wellbeing, which can support weight loss.

Reiki:

Reiki is a form of energy healing that involves the transfer of healing energy from the practitioner to the client. Reiki can be used to promote relaxation, reduce stress, and improve overall wellbeing. It can also be used to support weight management by reducing stress levels, which can contribute to weight gain.

Stress can cause the body to produce cortisol, a hormone that is associated with weight gain. By reducing stress levels through Reiki, it may be possible to reduce cortisol levels and support weight loss. Additionally, Reiki can be used to support healthy eating habits by promoting mindfulness and reducing emotional eating.

Visualization:

Visualization is a powerful tool for weight management. Visualization involves using the power of the mind to create a mental image of the desired outcome. For example, if a person wants to lose weight, they may visualize themselves at their ideal weight, feeling healthy and strong.

Visualization can be used to support weight management by creating a positive mindset and increasing motivation. By visualizing the desired outcome, it can be easier to stay motivated and focused on weight loss goals. Additionally, visualization can be used to reduce stress and promote relaxation, which can support weight loss.

Crystals:

Crystals are natural objects that are believed to have healing properties. They can be used in a variety of ways to support weight management. For example, rose quartz is a crystal that is associated with self-love and compassion. By carrying rose quartz with you or placing it in your environment, it may be possible to increase feelings of self-love and reduce negative self-talk, which can support weight loss.

Additionally, crystals can be used to promote overall health and wellbeing, which can support weight management. For example, amethyst is a crystal that is associated with relaxation and stress reduction. By carrying amethyst with you or placing it in your environment, it may be possible to reduce stress levels and promote relaxation, which can support healthy eating habits and weight loss.

Meditation:

Meditation is a practice that involves focusing the mind on a particular object or thought, in order to promote relaxation and reduce stress. Meditation can be used to support weight management by reducing stress levels and promoting mindfulness. By practicing meditation regularly, it may be possible to reduce emotional eating and increase awareness of the body's needs.

Meditation can also be used to promote a positive mindset and increase motivation for weight loss. By using affirmations during meditation, such as "I am healthy and strong", it can be easier to stay motivated and focused on weight loss goals.

Weight management can be a challenging journey, but energy healing can be a powerful tool for promoting weight loss, improving body image, and supporting overall health and wellness. Chakra balancing, Reiki, visualization, crystals, and meditation are just a few of the ways that energy healing can be used to support weight management.

By addressing the underlying emotional and spiritual factors that may contribute to weight gain, it may be possible to achieve long-term success in weight management. Energy healing can help to promote relaxation, reduce stress, increase self-love and compassion, and promote overall health and wellbeing, all of which can support weight loss and a healthy lifestyle.

If you are struggling with weight management, consider incorporating energy healing into your routine. Consult with an energy healing practitioner to learn more about how these techniques can support your weight loss goals and improve your overall health and wellbeing. Remember, weight management is a journey, and with the right tools and support, it is possible to achieve lasting success.

Part 6:
Healing the Spirit

Chapter 24: The Connection Between Energy and Spirit

The human spirit is a mysterious force that drives us to explore the depths of our existence. It is what gives us purpose and meaning in life, and connects us to something greater than ourselves. However, the spirit is not something that can be easily defined or understood. It is a complex entity that is shaped by our experiences, beliefs, and emotions.

Energy is another force that is closely intertwined with the spirit. It is the force that flows through all living things, connecting us to each other and the universe. The connection between energy and spirit is a complex one, and exploring this connection can lead us to a deeper understanding of ourselves and the world around us.

In this chapter, we will explore the connection between energy and spirit, and how this connection can be harnessed to promote healing and wellbeing.

What is Energy?

Energy is a force that is present in all living things. It is what drives our bodies and allows us to think, feel, and experience the world around us. Energy is not something that can be seen or touched, but it can be felt and harnessed.

There are many different types of energy, including kinetic energy (the energy of motion), potential energy (the energy of position), and thermal energy (the energy of heat). However, the type of energy that is most closely associated with the spirit is spiritual energy.

What is Spiritual Energy?

Spiritual energy is the energy that flows through all living things, connecting us to each other and the universe. It is what gives us a sense of purpose and meaning in life, and connects us to something greater than ourselves. Spiritual energy can be felt as a sense of peace, calm, and wellbeing.

Spiritual energy is often associated with spirituality and religion, but it is not limited to these areas. It is a force that is present in all living things, regardless of belief or background. It is the force that drives us to connect with others, to seek meaning and purpose in life, and to explore the depths of our existence.

The Connection Between Energy and Spirit

The connection between energy and spirit is a complex one. Energy is the force that drives the body, while spirit is the force that drives the soul. However, these two forces are closely intertwined, and one cannot exist without the other.

The connection between energy and spirit can be seen in the way that energy flows through the body. Energy flows through the body along pathways called meridians. These meridians are closely connected to the chakras, which are energy centers located throughout the body.

The chakras are associated with different aspects of physical, emotional, and spiritual health. For example, the root chakra, located at the base of the spine, is associated with issues of survival and security. If this chakra is blocked, it can contribute to feelings of anxiety and insecurity, which can impact both physical and emotional wellbeing.

By working to balance the chakras, it is possible to promote the flow of spiritual energy throughout the body. This can help to promote healing and wellbeing, and can lead to a deeper sense of connection with the world around us.

How to Harness the Connection Between Energy and Spirit

There are many different ways to harness the connection between energy and spirit. Here are some techniques that can be used to promote healing and wellbeing:

Meditation:

Meditation is a powerful tool for harnessing the connection between energy and spirit. It involves quieting the mind and focusing on the present moment. Through meditation, it is possible to tap into the spiritual energy that flows through all living things.

Meditation can be used to promote relaxation, reduce stress, and improve overall wellbeing. It can also be used to connect with the spiritual realm, and to explore the depths of the human spirit.

Yoga:

Yoga is another powerful tool for harnessing the connection between energy and spirit. It involves a series of physical poses, breathing techniques, and meditation practices that are designed to balance the chakras and promote the flow of spiritual energy throughout the body.

Yoga can be used to improve physical health, increase flexibility and strength, and promote relaxation and stress reduction. It can also be used to connect with the spiritual realm and to explore the depths of the human spirit.

Reiki:

Reiki is a healing technique that involves the use of spiritual energy to promote healing and wellbeing. It is based on the idea that the body has a natural ability to heal itself, and that this ability can be enhanced through the use of spiritual energy.

During a Reiki session, the practitioner will place their hands on or near the body of the client, using spiritual energy to promote healing and balance. Reiki can be used to promote physical healing, reduce stress and anxiety, and improve overall wellbeing.

Crystal Healing:

Crystal healing is a technique that involves the use of crystals to promote healing and balance. Crystals are believed to have their own unique energy, which can be used to balance the chakras and promote the flow of spiritual energy throughout the body.

During a crystal healing session, the practitioner will place crystals on or near the body of the client, using their energy to promote healing and balance. Crystal healing can be used to promote physical healing, reduce stress and anxiety, and improve overall wellbeing.

Sound Healing:

Sound healing is a technique that involves the use of sound to promote healing and balance. Sound is believed to have its own unique energy, which can be used to balance the chakras and promote the flow of spiritual energy throughout the body.

During a sound healing session, the practitioner will use different types of sound, such as singing bowls, gongs, or tuning forks, to promote healing and balance. Sound healing can be used to promote physical healing, reduce stress and anxiety, and improve overall wellbeing.

The connection between energy and spirit is a powerful one. It is what drives us to explore the depths of our existence, and to connect with something greater than ourselves. By harnessing this connection, it is possible to promote healing and wellbeing, and to connect with the spiritual realm.

There are many different techniques that can be used to harness the connection between energy and spirit, including meditation, yoga, Reiki, crystal healing, and sound healing. These techniques can be used to promote physical healing, reduce stress and anxiety, and improve overall wellbeing.

Ultimately, the connection between energy and spirit is a deeply personal one. It is something that each individual must explore for themselves, and that can be shaped by their own experiences, beliefs, and emotions. By embracing this connection, however, it is possible to find a deeper sense of purpose and meaning in life, and to connect with the universe in a powerful and profound way.

Chapter 25: Energy Healing for Spiritual Growth

Energy healing is a practice that has been used for thousands of years to promote physical, emotional, and spiritual healing. It is based on the concept that all living things are made up of energy, and that this energy can be influenced and manipulated to promote healing and wellbeing.

In this chapter, we will explore the connection between energy healing and spiritual growth, and how energy healing can be used to promote spiritual development and awareness.

The Connection Between Energy Healing and Spiritual Growth

Energy healing is a powerful tool for promoting spiritual growth and awareness. It works by manipulating the energy fields that surround and permeate the body, and by balancing the chakras and other energy centers.

When energy is blocked or stagnant in the body, it can lead to physical and emotional problems, as well as a feeling of disconnection from the spiritual realm. Energy healing can help to release these blockages and promote the flow of spiritual energy, leading to a deeper sense of connection with the world around us.

Energy Healing Techniques for Spiritual Growth

There are many different energy healing techniques that can be used to promote spiritual growth and awareness. Here are some of the most popular:

Reiki

Reiki is a Japanese healing technique that uses the hands to channel energy into the body. It is based on the concept that energy can be manipulated and directed to promote healing and wellbeing.

During a Reiki session, the practitioner places their hands on or near the body, and channels energy into the recipient. This energy helps to release blockages and promote the flow of spiritual energy, leading to a sense of calm, relaxation, and wellbeing.

Chakra Balancing

Chakras are energy centers located throughout the body that are associated with different aspects of physical, emotional, and spiritual health. When these chakras are balanced and flowing freely, it can promote spiritual growth and awareness.

Chakra balancing can be done through a variety of techniques, including meditation, visualization, and the use of crystals and essential oils. By focusing on each chakra and promoting balance and flow, it is possible to promote spiritual growth and awareness.

Crystal Healing

Crystals are powerful tools for promoting spiritual growth and awareness. They are believed to have unique properties that can help to balance the body's energy fields and promote healing and wellbeing.

During a crystal healing session, the practitioner places different types of crystals on or near the body, and channels energy into the crystals. This energy helps to release blockages and promote the flow of spiritual energy, leading to a sense of calm, relaxation, and wellbeing.

Sound Healing

Sound healing is a technique that uses sound to promote healing and wellbeing. It is based on the concept that sound vibrations can influence the body's energy fields, promoting balance and flow.

During a sound healing session, the practitioner uses a variety of instruments, such as singing bowls or gongs, to produce sound vibrations. These vibrations help to release blockages and promote the flow of spiritual energy, leading to a sense of calm, relaxation, and wellbeing.

Benefits of Energy Healing for Spiritual Growth

Energy healing has many benefits for spiritual growth and awareness. Here are some of the most significant:

Promotes relaxation and stress reduction

Energy healing can help to promote relaxation and reduce stress, which can be a significant obstacle to spiritual growth and awareness. By promoting a sense of calm and relaxation, energy healing can help to quiet the mind and open up the channels of spiritual energy.

Increases awareness of the spiritual realm

Energy healing can help to increase awareness of the spiritual realm, and promote a deeper sense of connection with the world around us. By promoting the flow of spiritual energy, energy healing can help to awaken the senses and promote spiritual growth and awareness.

Promotes emotional healing

Energy healing can help to promote emotional healing, which is a crucial component of spiritual growth. By releasing emotional blockages and promoting a sense of emotional balance, energy healing can help us to move past negative patterns and emotions that can hold us back from spiritual growth.

Enhances intuition and inner wisdom

As energy healing promotes a deeper connection with our spiritual selves, it can also help to enhance our intuition and inner wisdom. By promoting a sense of calm and relaxation, energy healing can help us to quiet the mind and connect more deeply with our inner selves, allowing us to access our own inner wisdom.

Promotes physical healing

While energy healing is often associated with spiritual and emotional healing, it can also have physical benefits. By promoting the flow of energy throughout the body, energy healing can help to stimulate the body's natural healing processes and promote physical health and wellbeing.

Overall, energy healing can be a powerful tool for promoting spiritual growth and awareness. By promoting relaxation, increasing awareness of the spiritual realm, promoting emotional healing, enhancing intuition and inner wisdom, and promoting physical healing, energy healing can help us to connect more deeply with our spiritual selves and live more fulfilling lives.

Chapter 26: Connecting with Your Higher Self

In this chapter, we will explore the concept of the Higher Self, and how you can connect with this powerful inner guide to promote spiritual growth and awareness.

The Higher Self

The Higher Self is a concept that has been explored by many spiritual traditions and philosophies. It is the part of us that is connected to the divine, and it is said to be the source of our intuition, wisdom, and spiritual guidance.

The Higher Self is often described as a wise and loving guide that is always with us, offering us guidance and support on our spiritual journey. It is said to be the part of us that is connected to the universe, and it is believed to be the source of our true purpose and potential.

Connecting with Your Higher Self

Connecting with your Higher Self is a powerful way to promote spiritual growth and awareness. Here are some techniques that you can use to connect with this inner guide:

Meditation

Meditation is one of the most powerful ways to connect with your Higher Self. By quieting the mind and turning your attention inward, you can access the wisdom and guidance of your inner guide.

To meditate, find a quiet and comfortable place where you can sit undisturbed for a period of time. Close your eyes and focus your attention on your breath. If your mind wanders, gently bring it back to your breath.

As you continue to meditate, allow yourself to connect with your Higher Self. Visualize a loving and wise presence within you, and ask for guidance and support on your spiritual journey. Listen for any insights or messages that come to you.

Journaling

Journaling is another powerful tool for connecting with your Higher Self. By putting your thoughts and feelings on paper, you can access deeper levels of insight and understanding.

To journal, find a quiet and comfortable place where you can write undisturbed for a period of time. Set an intention to connect with your Higher Self, and then begin writing. Allow yourself to write freely and without judgment.

As you write, allow yourself to connect with your inner guide. Ask for guidance and support on your spiritual journey, and listen for any insights or messages that come to you.

Visualization

Visualization is a powerful way to connect with your Higher Self. By using your imagination to create vivid mental images, you can access deeper levels of insight and understanding.

To visualize, find a quiet and comfortable place where you can sit undisturbed for a period of time. Close your eyes and visualize a loving and wise presence within you. Allow yourself to connect with this inner guide, and ask for guidance and support on your spiritual journey.

As you continue to visualize, allow yourself to explore any insights or messages that come to you. Use your imagination to create vivid mental images of your spiritual path, and allow yourself to connect with the deeper wisdom and guidance of your Higher Self.

Movement

Movement is another powerful way to connect with your Higher Self. By using your body to express your inner wisdom and guidance, you can access deeper levels of insight and understanding.

To use movement to connect with your Higher Self, find a quiet and comfortable place where you can move freely. Begin by focusing your attention on your breath, and then allow yourself to move freely and without judgment.

As you move, allow yourself to connect with your inner guide. Ask for guidance and support on your spiritual journey, and allow yourself to express your inner wisdom and guidance through your movements.

Benefits of Connecting with Your Higher Self

Connecting with your Higher Self has many benefits for spiritual growth and awareness. Here are some of the most significant:

Promotes spiritual growth and awareness

Connecting with your Higher Self can help to promote spiritual growth and awareness by providing you with guidance and support on your spiritual journey.

Increases intuition and insight

Connecting with your Higher Self can also increase your intuition and insight, allowing you to tap into your inner wisdom and make more informed decisions in your life.

Enhances creativity

When you connect with your Higher Self, you tap into a wellspring of creativity and inspiration that can help you to express yourself more fully in your creative pursuits.

Promotes inner peace and calm

Connecting with your Higher Self can also promote a sense of inner peace and calm, as you learn to trust in the guidance and support that is always available to you.

Deepens your sense of purpose and meaning

By connecting with your Higher Self, you can tap into a deeper sense of purpose and meaning in your life, as you discover your true calling and align yourself with your highest potential.

Connecting with your Higher Self is a powerful way to promote spiritual growth and awareness, and to tap into the inner wisdom and guidance that is always available to you. By using techniques such as meditation, journaling, visualization, and movement, you can deepen your connection to this inner guide, and experience the many benefits that come with it. As you continue on your spiritual journey, remember to stay open and receptive to the insights and messages that come from your Higher Self, and trust in the guidance and support that is always available to you.

Chapter 27: Cultivating Your Inner Wisdom

In our busy lives, it can be easy to lose touch with our inner wisdom. We may become so caught up in our daily routines and responsibilities that we forget to listen to the voice within us that knows what is best for us.

However, our inner wisdom is always present, waiting to be cultivated and accessed. In this chapter, we will explore how to cultivate your inner wisdom and access the guidance and insight that lies within you.

What is Inner Wisdom?

Inner wisdom is the part of us that knows what is best for us. It is the part of us that is connected to our intuition, our deepest desires, and our highest purpose.

Unlike our conscious mind, which is often clouded by external influences and distractions, our inner wisdom is always present and always available to us. It speaks to us through our intuition, our dreams, and our gut feelings.

Cultivating Your Inner Wisdom

Cultivating your inner wisdom requires practice and patience. Here are some techniques that you can use to connect with your inner wisdom and cultivate a deeper understanding of yourself.

Listen to Your Intuition

Your intuition is your inner guidance system. It is the voice within you that knows what is best for you, even when your conscious mind is uncertain.

To listen to your intuition, pay attention to the messages that you receive from within. Notice any gut feelings, hunches, or instincts that you have. Trust that these feelings are valid and that they are guiding you towards what is best for you.

Practice Mindfulness

Mindfulness is the practice of being present and fully engaged in the current moment. When we are mindful, we are able to quiet our minds and tune in to our inner wisdom.

To practice mindfulness, find a quiet and comfortable place where you can sit undisturbed for a period of time. Close your eyes and focus your attention on your breath. If your mind wanders, gently bring it back to your breath.

As you continue to practice mindfulness, allow yourself to connect with your inner wisdom. Notice any insights or messages that come to you.

Journal

Journaling is a powerful tool for accessing your inner wisdom. By putting your thoughts and feelings on paper, you can gain a deeper understanding of yourself and the guidance that lies within you.

To journal, find a quiet and comfortable place where you can write undisturbed for a period of time. Set an intention to connect with your inner wisdom, and then begin writing. Allow yourself to write freely and without judgment.

As you write, notice any insights or messages that come to you. Trust that these messages are coming from your inner wisdom and that they are guiding you towards what is best for you.

Connect with Nature

Nature has a way of quieting our minds and allowing us to connect with our inner wisdom. When we are in nature, we are able to tune in to the rhythms of the earth and connect with the wisdom that lies within us.

To connect with nature, find a quiet and peaceful outdoor space where you can be alone. Take a walk, sit by a stream, or simply spend time in the natural world. As you do so, allow yourself to connect with your inner wisdom and notice any insights or messages that come to you.

Practice Self-Care

Self-care is an essential part of cultivating your inner wisdom. When we take care of ourselves, we are able to quiet our minds and connect with our inner guidance.

To practice self-care, make time for activities that nourish your body, mind, and spirit. This may include getting enough sleep, eating a healthy diet, exercising, spending time with loved ones, and engaging in activities that bring you joy.

As you practice self-care, notice how it feels to connect with your inner wisdom. You may find that when you take care of yourself, you are better able to access the guidance and insight that lies within you.

Embrace Your Emotions

Our emotions are a powerful tool for accessing our inner wisdom. When we allow ourselves to feel our emotions, we are able to connect with the deeper parts of ourselves and gain a deeper understanding of our needs and desires.

To embrace your emotions, give yourself permission to feel. Allow yourself to feel whatever emotions come up, without judgment or resistance. Notice where you feel these emotions in your body, and allow yourself to fully experience them.

As you embrace your emotions, pay attention to any insights or messages that come to you. Trust that these emotions are guiding you towards what is best for you.

Trust Yourself

Ultimately, cultivating your inner wisdom requires trust. You must trust yourself and your own inner guidance.

To trust yourself, practice listening to your intuition and following your gut. When you receive messages from within, trust that they are valid and that they are guiding you towards what is best for you.

Remember, your inner wisdom is always present and always available to you. By cultivating your inner wisdom, you can access the guidance and insight that lies within you, and live a life that is aligned with your deepest desires and highest purpose.

Part 7:

Energy Healing for Relationships

Chapter 28: The Connection Between Energy and Relationships

Our relationships are an integral part of our lives. They can bring us joy, companionship, and support. However, relationships can also be a source of stress, conflict, and negativity. What many people don't realize is that there is a deep connection between our energy and our relationships. In this chapter, we will explore the connection between energy and relationships and how we can cultivate positive energy in our relationships.

Understanding Energy

Everything in the universe is made up of energy, including ourselves and our relationships. Energy is the invisible force that flows through us and connects us to everything around us. We are all vibrational beings, and our energy frequencies can affect our lives and relationships.

Negative energy can cause us to feel drained, anxious, and stressed, while positive energy can uplift and inspire us. Our energy is constantly changing and influenced by our thoughts, emotions, and environment.

Energy in Relationships

Our relationships are a reflection of our energy. When we are in a positive state of mind and have high energy, our relationships tend to be positive and uplifting. Conversely, when we are in a negative state of mind and have low energy, our relationships can become strained and difficult.

Have you ever noticed how you feel after spending time with certain people? Some people may leave you feeling energized and inspired, while others may leave you feeling drained and depleted. This is because their energy frequencies are either in alignment or out of alignment with yours.

When our energy frequencies are in alignment, we feel a sense of connection and resonance with others. We are able to communicate effectively and resolve conflicts in a constructive way. However, when our energy frequencies are out of alignment, we may experience tension, conflict, and misunderstandings.

Cultivating Positive Energy in Relationships

Cultivating positive energy in our relationships requires conscious effort and awareness. Here are some techniques that can help you cultivate positive energy in your relationships:

Practice Mindfulness

Mindfulness is the practice of being present and fully engaged in the current moment. When we are mindful, we are able to quiet our minds and tune in to our energy.

To practice mindfulness, find a quiet and comfortable place where you can sit undisturbed for a period of time. Close your eyes and focus your attention on your breath. If your mind wanders, gently bring it back to your breath.

As you continue to practice mindfulness, allow yourself to connect with your energy. Notice any feelings or sensations that arise within you.

Set Intentions

Setting intentions is a powerful way to cultivate positive energy in your relationships. When we set intentions, we are directing our energy towards a specific outcome.

To set intentions, take some time to reflect on what you want to create in your relationships. Ask yourself what kind of energy you want to bring to your relationships, and how you want to feel in your interactions with others.

Write your intentions down and place them somewhere where you can see them daily. As you go about your day, keep your intentions in mind and allow them to guide your thoughts and actions.

Practice Gratitude

Gratitude is a powerful way to cultivate positive energy in our relationships. When we are grateful, we are able to shift our focus from what is lacking to what is abundant in our lives.

To practice gratitude, take some time each day to reflect on what you are grateful for in your relationships. This could be as simple as appreciating someone's kindness or acknowledging a small act of love.

Express your gratitude to others by telling them how much you appreciate them. This will not only uplift their energy, but also reinforce positive energy in your relationships.

Set Boundaries

Setting boundaries is an important way to protect your energy in relationships. Boundaries are a way of communicating your needs and ensuring that your energy is not depleted by others.

To set boundaries, take some time to reflect on what you need in your relationships to feel safe, respected, and valued. Communicate your boundaries clearly and assertively, and be willing to enforce them when necessary.

Setting boundaries can be challenging, but it is essential for maintaining positive energy in your relationships. When you allow others to cross your boundaries, you are essentially allowing them to drain your energy and compromise your well-being.

Forgiveness

Forgiveness is a powerful way to release negative energy in our relationships. When we hold onto resentment and anger towards others, we are essentially holding onto negative energy that can impact our relationships and overall well-being.

To practice forgiveness, begin by acknowledging your feelings towards the person who has hurt you. Allow yourself to feel the emotions that come up, but also be willing to let them go.

Reflect on the situation and try to understand the other person's perspective. This doesn't mean that you have to condone their behavior, but rather, it is about gaining empathy and compassion for them.

Finally, forgive them. This doesn't mean that you have to forget what they have done or reconcile with them, but rather, it is about releasing the negative energy and moving forward with a sense of peace and freedom.

Our relationships are an essential part of our lives, and they have a significant impact on our energy and overall well-being. By cultivating positive energy in our relationships, we can experience greater joy, love, and fulfillment.

Remember that everything is energy, and our thoughts, emotions, and actions all have a vibrational frequency that can affect our relationships. By practicing mindfulness, setting intentions, expressing gratitude, setting boundaries, and practicing forgiveness, we can cultivate positive energy and transform our relationships.

So take some time to reflect on your relationships and ask yourself how you can cultivate positive energy in them. Remember that it takes conscious effort and awareness, but the rewards are well worth it.

Chapter 29: Healing Relationship Wounds with Energy Healing

Relationships are a vital part of our lives, and they can bring us immense joy, love, and happiness. However, relationships can also be a source of pain, heartache, and trauma. When we experience hurt or trauma in our relationships, it can leave us feeling wounded and vulnerable. These wounds can affect us not only emotionally, but also physically and energetically.

Energy healing is a powerful tool that can help us heal the wounds of our past relationships and cultivate positive, healthy connections in our present and future relationships. In this chapter, we will explore how energy healing can support our healing journey and help us transform our relationships.

Understanding Relationship Wounds

Relationship wounds are the emotional, physical, and energetic scars that we carry from past relationships. These wounds can manifest in various ways, such as trust issues, fear of intimacy, difficulty in setting boundaries, and low self-esteem. They can also affect our physical health, causing chronic pain, tension, and illness.

Relationship wounds can be caused by various factors, including childhood trauma, past abuse, neglect, abandonment, and betrayal. These wounds can be deeply ingrained in our subconscious, and we may not even be aware of their existence until they start affecting our relationships.

Healing Relationship Wounds with Energy Healing

Energy healing is a holistic approach to healing that addresses the root cause of our physical, emotional, and energetic imbalances. It involves using various techniques to balance and harmonize our energy fields, release emotional blockages, and promote self-healing.

Here are some energy healing techniques that can help us heal our relationship wounds:

Chakra Healing

Chakras are the energy centers in our body that regulate the flow of energy. When our chakras are balanced and aligned, we experience optimal health and well-being. However, when our chakras are blocked or imbalanced, we may experience physical, emotional, and energetic issues.

Healing our chakras can help us release emotional blockages and heal our relationship wounds. Each chakra is associated with different emotions and aspects of our life, and healing them can help us address specific issues related to our relationships.

For example, the heart chakra is associated with love, compassion, and relationships. When our heart chakra is imbalanced, we may experience issues with trust, intimacy, and connection in our relationships. Healing our heart chakra can help us release emotional wounds and open ourselves up to love and connection.

Reiki Healing

Reiki is a Japanese technique for stress reduction and relaxation that also promotes healing. It involves using the hands to channel energy into the body to activate the natural healing processes.

Reiki can help us release emotional and energetic blockages and promote healing in our relationships. It can help us release negative energy and emotions from past relationships and cultivate positive energy and connection in our current relationships.

Reiki can also help us release stress and anxiety, which can affect our relationships negatively. By promoting relaxation and inner peace, Reiki can help us show up as our best selves in our relationships.

EFT (Emotional Freedom Technique)

EFT is a powerful energy healing technique that involves tapping on specific points on the body to release emotional blockages. It can help us release negative emotions and beliefs that are holding us back in our relationships.

EFT can help us address specific relationship wounds, such as trust issues, fear of intimacy, and low self-esteem. By tapping on these specific issues, we can release the emotional charge and create space for healing and transformation.

Sound Healing

Sound healing involves using sound frequencies to balance and harmonize our energy fields. It can help us release emotional blockages and promote healing in our relationships.

Sound healing can be especially effective in releasing emotional trauma and promoting emotional release. By listening to specific sound frequencies, we can activate our body's natural healing processes and release emotional and energetic blockages.

Sound healing can also help us cultivate positive energy and connection in our relationships. By listening to soothing and calming sounds, we can promote relaxation and inner peace, which can help us show up as our best selves in our relationships.

How Energy Healing Can Transform Our Relationships

Energy healing can help us transform our relationships in many ways. Here are some of the ways in which energy healing can support our healing journey and help us cultivate positive, healthy connections in our relationships:

Healing Emotional Wounds: Energy healing can help us release emotional wounds from past relationships and promote healing. By addressing the root cause of our emotional pain, we can create space for healing and transformation.

Cultivating Positive Energy: Energy healing can help us cultivate positive energy and connection in our relationships. By releasing negative energy and emotions, we can create space for positive energy and connection to flow.

Building Trust: Trust is a vital component of healthy relationships. Energy healing can help us release trust issues and build trust in our relationships.

Enhancing Intimacy: Intimacy is an essential aspect of healthy relationships. Energy healing can help us release fear of intimacy and cultivate deeper intimacy and connection in our relationships.

Setting Boundaries: Setting boundaries is an important part of healthy relationships. Energy healing can help us release issues with setting boundaries and cultivate healthy boundaries in our relationships.

Boosting Self-Esteem: Self-esteem is a crucial factor in healthy relationships. Energy healing can help us release low self-esteem and cultivate self-love and confidence.

Letting Go of Past Relationships: Letting go of past relationships is essential for moving forward and creating positive, healthy connections in our present and future relationships. Energy healing can help us release emotional attachments and let go of past relationships.

Relationship wounds can affect us in many ways, emotionally, physically, and energetically. Energy healing is a powerful tool that can help us heal our relationship wounds and cultivate positive, healthy connections in our relationships.

Through techniques such as chakra healing, Reiki healing, EFT, and sound healing, we can release emotional blockages, cultivate positive energy, and transform our relationships. By addressing the root cause of our emotional pain, we can create space for healing and transformation, and build trust, intimacy, and healthy boundaries in our relationships.

With energy healing, we can let go of past relationships, boost our self-esteem, and show up as our best selves in our relationships. By cultivating positive energy and connection, we can experience the joy, love, and happiness that healthy relationships bring into our lives.

Chapter 30: Using Energy Healing to Strengthen Relationships

Relationships are an essential aspect of our lives. They can bring us immense joy, love, and happiness, and they can also be a source of pain, heartache, and trauma. We all desire to have healthy, fulfilling relationships that nourish us and help us grow, but achieving this can be challenging.

Energy healing is a powerful tool that can help us strengthen our relationships and cultivate deeper connections with our loved ones. In this chapter, we will explore how energy healing can support us in building strong, healthy relationships.

Understanding Relationship Dynamics

Before we dive into energy healing techniques for strengthening relationships, it's essential to understand relationship dynamics. Relationships are complex, and there are many factors that influence their success, including communication, trust, vulnerability, and respect.

To build strong, healthy relationships, we need to create a foundation of trust, respect, and open communication. We must also be willing to be vulnerable and share our true selves with our loved ones.

However, this can be challenging, as we often carry emotional baggage from past relationships that can hinder our ability to connect authentically. We may have trust issues, fear of intimacy, difficulty in setting boundaries, and low self-esteem, all of which can impact our ability to form healthy relationships.

Energy Healing Techniques for Strengthening Relationships

Energy healing can help us release emotional blockages and promote healing in our relationships. Here are some energy healing techniques that can help us strengthen our relationships:

Reiki Healing

Reiki is a Japanese technique for stress reduction and relaxation that also promotes healing. It involves using the hands to channel energy into the body to activate the natural healing processes.

Reiki can be particularly effective in promoting emotional healing and releasing negative energy from past relationships. It can help us release emotional baggage and create space for healing and transformation.

Reiki can also help us cultivate positive energy and connection in our current relationships. It can promote relaxation and inner peace, helping us show up as our best selves in our relationships.

Chakra Healing

Chakras are the energy centers in our body that regulate the flow of energy. When our chakras are balanced and aligned, we experience optimal health and well-being.

Chakra healing can help us release emotional blockages and promote healing in our relationships. Each chakra is associated with different emotions and aspects of our life, and healing them can help us address specific issues related to our relationships.

For example, the heart chakra is associated with love, compassion, and relationships. When our heart chakra is imbalanced, we may experience issues with trust, intimacy, and connection in our relationships. Healing our heart chakra can help us release emotional wounds and open ourselves up to love and connection.

Mindfulness Meditation

Mindfulness meditation is a powerful technique for cultivating awareness and presence in the present moment. It involves focusing our attention on our breath, sensations in the body, and thoughts and emotions as they arise.

Mindfulness meditation can help us become more aware of our thoughts and emotions and how they impact our relationships. It can also help us cultivate empathy and compassion, which are essential qualities for building healthy relationships.

Mindfulness meditation can also help us manage stress and anxiety, which can negatively impact our relationships. By promoting relaxation and inner peace, mindfulness meditation can help us show up as our best selves in our relationships.

Gratitude Practice

Gratitude is a powerful tool for cultivating positive energy and promoting healing in our relationships. When we focus on what we're grateful for, we shift our energy from lack to abundance, which can help us attract more positivity into our lives.

Practicing gratitude can help us cultivate appreciation for our loved ones and strengthen our relationships. It can also help us shift our perspective from negative to positive, which can help us overcome relationship challenges more easily.

Steps for Using Energy Healing to Strengthen Relationships

Now that we have explored some energy healing techniques for strengthening relationships let's look at some specific steps we can take to incorporate these techniques into our daily lives.

Step 1: Identify Your Relationship Goals

To start using energy healing to strengthen our relationships, we must first identify our relationship goals. What kind of relationships do we want to cultivate? What qualities do we want to embody in our relationships? What challenges do we want to overcome?

By identifying our relationship goals, we create a clear intention for our energy healing practice. This intention will guide us in selecting the appropriate energy healing techniques and practices for our specific needs.

Step 2: Practice Daily Self-Care

Self-care is essential for cultivating healthy relationships. When we take care of ourselves, we show up as our best selves in our relationships, which can help us build deeper connections with our loved ones.

Incorporating energy healing practices into our daily self-care routine can help us promote emotional healing, release negative energy, and cultivate positive energy in our relationships.

We can start by practicing Reiki or chakra healing on ourselves regularly to release emotional blockages and promote healing in our relationships. We can also practice mindfulness meditation to become more aware of our thoughts and emotions and cultivate empathy and compassion.

Step 3: Communicate Effectively

Effective communication is essential for building healthy relationships. We must be willing to listen actively to our loved ones, express ourselves authentically, and communicate our needs and boundaries clearly.

Energy healing can help us cultivate open communication in our relationships by releasing emotional blockages that may be hindering our ability to express ourselves authentically.

We can start by practicing mindfulness meditation to become more aware of our thoughts and emotions and how they impact our communication with others. We can also practice Reiki or chakra healing to release emotional wounds and promote healing in our relationships, which can help us show up more authentically in our communication with others.

Step 4: Cultivate Gratitude and Positivity

Gratitude and positivity are powerful tools for strengthening relationships. When we focus on what we're grateful for, we shift our energy from lack to abundance, which can help us attract more positivity into our lives.

We can start by practicing a daily gratitude practice, where we focus on what we're grateful for in our relationships. This can help us cultivate appreciation for our loved ones and strengthen our connections with them.

We can also practice Reiki or chakra healing to promote positive energy and connection in our relationships. By cultivating positive energy, we can attract more positivity into our lives and strengthen our relationships.

Step 5: Seek Professional Support

Sometimes, despite our best efforts, we may still struggle with building healthy relationships. In such cases, seeking professional support from a therapist or energy healer can be helpful.

Professional support can help us identify and address underlying emotional blockages that may be hindering our ability to form healthy relationships. A therapist or energy healer can also provide us with personalized energy healing techniques and practices to help us cultivate deeper connections with our loved ones.

In conclusion, energy healing can be a powerful tool for strengthening relationships. By promoting emotional healing, releasing negative energy, and cultivating positive energy, energy healing can help us build stronger, healthier relationships with our loved ones.

To incorporate energy healing into our daily lives, we can start by practicing Reiki or chakra healing, mindfulness meditation, and gratitude practice regularly. We can also communicate effectively with our loved ones, cultivate positivity and gratitude, and seek professional support when needed.

Remember, building healthy relationships takes time and effort, but with the right energy healing practices, we can cultivate deeper connections with our loved ones and experience more joy, love, and happiness in our lives.

Chapter 31: Cultivating Love and Compassion with Energy Healing

Love and compassion are two of the most powerful forces in the universe. They have the power to heal, transform, and uplift us, and they can help us create a better world for ourselves and others.

Energy healing is a powerful tool that can help us cultivate love and compassion in our lives. In this chapter, we will explore how energy healing can support us in cultivating love and compassion.

Understanding Love and Compassion

Love and compassion are often used interchangeably, but they are two distinct qualities. Love is the feeling of deep affection and connection towards oneself and others. Compassion is the quality of being able to understand and empathize with the suffering of others and to take action to alleviate it.

Both love and compassion are essential qualities for our personal growth and spiritual development. They help us cultivate inner peace, joy, and happiness and connect us with the world around us.

However, cultivating love and compassion can be challenging, particularly in a world that can be filled with negativity, fear, and suffering. We may struggle with feelings of anger, resentment, and fear, which can hinder our ability to connect with others and cultivate love and compassion.

Energy Healing Techniques for Cultivating Love and Compassion

Energy healing can help us release emotional blockages and promote healing in our lives, allowing us to cultivate love and compassion. Here are some energy healing techniques that can help us cultivate love and compassion:

Heart Meditation

Heart meditation is a powerful technique for opening the heart chakra, the energy center that regulates love, compassion, and relationships. It involves focusing our attention on the heart center and visualizing love and compassion flowing in and out of our hearts.

Heart meditation can help us cultivate love and compassion for ourselves and others. It can also help us release emotional blockages that may be hindering our ability to connect with others and cultivate these qualities.

Heart meditation can also help us cultivate forgiveness and compassion towards ourselves and others. It can help us release feelings of anger, resentment, and fear and replace them with love and compassion.

Metaphysical Healing

Metaphysical healing is a form of energy healing that involves working with the subtle energies that make up our bodies and the universe. It involves using intention and visualization to promote healing and transformation.

Metaphysical healing can help us cultivate love and compassion by releasing emotional blockages and promoting healing in our bodies and minds. It can also help us connect with the universe and the divine, which can help us cultivate a sense of oneness and interconnectedness with all beings.

One form of metaphysical healing is called the Violet Flame, which is a powerful tool for transmuting negative energy into positive energy. The

Violet Flame can help us release negative emotions and thoughts and replace them with love and compassion.

Crystal Healing

Crystal healing is a form of energy healing that involves using crystals and gemstones to promote healing and balance in our bodies and minds. Different crystals have different energetic properties and can be used to address specific issues and promote specific qualities.

Crystals such as rose quartz, amethyst, and clear quartz are particularly effective for promoting love and compassion. Rose quartz is known as the stone of love and can help us cultivate love and compassion for ourselves and others. Amethyst is known for its calming and balancing properties and can help us release emotional blockages that may be hindering our ability to connect with others. Clear quartz is a powerful amplifier of energy and can help us magnify our intentions for love and compassion.

Gratitude Practice

Gratitude is a powerful tool for cultivating positive energy and promoting healing in our lives. When we focus on what we're grateful for, we shift our energy from lack to abundance, which can help us attract more positivity into our lives.

Practicing gratitude can help us cultivate love and compassion for ourselves and others. It can also help us shift our perspective and focus on the positive aspects of our lives, which can improve our overall well-being.

To practice gratitude, simply take a few moments each day to reflect on what you're grateful for. You can write these down in a journal or simply reflect on them in your mind. You can also express your gratitude to others by thanking them for their presence in your life.

Reiki Healing

Reiki is a form of energy healing that involves channeling universal life force energy to promote healing and balance in the body and mind. It involves using gentle touch or placing the hands near the body to transfer energy to the recipient.

Reiki can help us release emotional blockages and promote healing in our bodies and minds. It can also help us cultivate love and compassion by promoting a sense of relaxation and inner peace.

During a Reiki session, the practitioner will place their hands on or near various energy centers in the body to promote balance and healing. The energy transfer can help us release negative emotions and promote positive ones, allowing us to cultivate love and compassion.

Cultivating love and compassion is an essential part of our personal growth and spiritual development. It can help us connect with ourselves and others, promote healing and balance in our lives, and create a better world for ourselves and others.

Energy healing techniques can be a powerful tool for cultivating love and compassion. Heart meditation, metaphysical healing, crystal healing, gratitude practice, and Reiki healing are all effective techniques for promoting healing and balance in our bodies and minds, allowing us to cultivate love and compassion.

By incorporating these energy healing techniques into our daily lives, we can release emotional blockages and promote healing and transformation, allowing us to connect with ourselves and others in a more loving and compassionate way.

Part 8:
Living a Balanced Life

Chapter 32: The Importance of Balance for Energy Healing

Balance is a fundamental principle of energy healing. It is the state of being in which all aspects of our being are in harmony, including our physical, emotional, mental, and spiritual bodies. When we are balanced, we are able to flow with the natural rhythms of life and experience a sense of peace, joy, and fulfillment.

In this chapter, we will explore the importance of balance for energy healing and how we can cultivate balance in our lives.

The Importance of Balance

Balance is essential for energy healing because it is the foundation for optimal health and well-being. When our energy is out of balance, we may experience physical, emotional, mental, or spiritual symptoms such as stress, anxiety, depression, chronic pain, or illness.

When we are in balance, our energy flows freely, and we are able to experience a sense of vitality, clarity, and inner peace. We are also able to access our innate healing power and promote healing in all aspects of our being.

Balance is not a static state, but a dynamic process that requires ongoing attention and care. We need to cultivate balance in all aspects of our being and align ourselves with the natural rhythms of life to maintain optimal health and well-being.

Cultivating Balance

Cultivating balance requires a holistic approach that addresses all aspects of our being, including our physical, emotional, mental, and spiritual bodies. Here are some practices that can help us cultivate balance:

Physical Balance

Physical balance is the foundation for all other aspects of our being. It is essential to maintain a healthy diet, regular exercise, and adequate rest to promote physical balance.

Eating a balanced diet that includes whole, nutrient-dense foods can help us maintain optimal physical health. Regular exercise can help us reduce stress, boost our immune system, and promote overall well-being. Adequate rest and sleep are also essential for physical balance, as they allow our bodies to repair and regenerate.

Emotional Balance

Emotional balance is essential for our mental and physical well-being. It involves being aware of our emotions and responding to them in a healthy and constructive way.

One practice for cultivating emotional balance is mindfulness meditation, which involves being present in the moment and observing our thoughts and emotions without judgment. This practice can help us become more aware of our emotions and respond to them in a healthy and constructive way.

Another practice for cultivating emotional balance is journaling, which involves writing down our thoughts and emotions. This practice can help us process our emotions and gain insight into our inner world.

Mental Balance

Mental balance involves having a clear and focused mind. It requires us to cultivate positive thoughts and attitudes and to release negative thought patterns.

One practice for cultivating mental balance is affirmations, which involve repeating positive statements to ourselves. This practice can help us shift our thought patterns from negative to positive and cultivate a more optimistic outlook on life.

Another practice for cultivating mental balance is visualization, which involves using our imagination to create positive mental images. This practice can help us create a clear vision for our lives and cultivate a sense of purpose and direction.

Spiritual Balance

Spiritual balance involves connecting with our innermost selves and with the divine. It requires us to cultivate a sense of purpose, meaning, and connection.

One practice for cultivating spiritual balance is prayer or meditation. This practice can help us connect with a higher power and cultivate a sense of peace and inner harmony.

Another practice for cultivating spiritual balance is spending time in nature. This practice can help us connect with the natural world and cultivate a sense of awe and wonder.

The Benefits of Balance

When we cultivate balance in all aspects of our being, we are able to experience a wide range of benefits. Here are some of the benefits of balance:

Improved physical health and well-being

Reduced stress and anxiety

Enhanced mental clarity and focus

Increased creativity and productivity

Greater emotional resilience

Increased spiritual awareness and connection

Improved relationships with others

Greater sense of purpose and fulfillment in life

In addition to these benefits, cultivating balance can also promote energy healing by allowing us to access our innate healing power. When we are in balance, our energy flows freely, and we are able to promote healing in all aspects of our being.

Tips for Maintaining Balance

Maintaining balance requires ongoing attention and care. Here are some tips for maintaining balance in your life:

Make self-care a priority: Take time for yourself each day to engage in activities that promote balance, such as meditation, exercise, or time in nature.

Set boundaries: Learn to say no to activities or people that drain your energy and set boundaries to protect your time and energy.

Practice mindfulness: Stay present in the moment and be aware of your thoughts, emotions, and physical sensations.

Cultivate gratitude: Focus on the good in your life and cultivate a sense of gratitude for all that you have.

Practice forgiveness: Let go of anger and resentment towards yourself and others and cultivate a spirit of forgiveness.

Balance is a fundamental principle of energy healing. It is the foundation for optimal health and well-being, allowing us to access our innate healing power and promote healing in all aspects of our being.

Cultivating balance requires a holistic approach that addresses all aspects of our being, including our physical, emotional, mental, and spiritual bodies. By making self-care a priority, setting boundaries, practicing mindfulness, cultivating gratitude, and practicing forgiveness, we can maintain balance in our lives and promote energy healing.

Remember, balance is not a static state, but a dynamic process that requires ongoing attention and care. By aligning ourselves with the natural rhythms of life and cultivating balance in all aspects of our being, we can experience a sense of peace, joy, and fulfillment in our lives.

Chapter 33: Finding Balance in Work and Life

In today's fast-paced world, finding balance between work and life can be a challenge. With the demands of work and the pressures of everyday life, it's easy to become overwhelmed and stressed. However, finding balance is crucial to our well-being and happiness.

In this chapter, we'll explore the importance of finding balance in work and life, and offer some practical tips for achieving it.

Why is Balance Important?

Finding balance between work and life is essential for our physical, mental, and emotional health. When we're constantly focused on work or other responsibilities, we may neglect other aspects of our lives, such as our relationships, hobbies, and self-care. This can lead to burnout, stress, and even physical illness.

On the other hand, when we prioritize our personal lives, we may neglect our work and professional goals, which can lead to financial stress and career stagnation.

Finding balance between work and life is about integrating all aspects of our lives in a way that allows us to thrive both personally and professionally. It's about creating a sense of harmony and flow that supports our overall well-being.

Tips for Finding Balance

Here are some practical tips for finding balance between work and life:

Set boundaries: Setting boundaries is essential for creating balance. It's important to establish clear boundaries between work and personal time, and to honor those boundaries. This may mean turning off your work phone after hours, avoiding work emails on the weekends, or simply saying no to additional work responsibilities that encroach on your personal time.

Prioritize self-care: Self-care is essential for maintaining balance. Prioritizing activities such as exercise, meditation, and time with loved ones can help us recharge and reduce stress. It's important to schedule time for self-care activities and to treat them as non-negotiable.

Use technology wisely: Technology can be a double-edged sword when it comes to finding balance. While it can make work more efficient, it can also be a source of distraction and stress. It's important to use technology wisely by setting boundaries on its use and avoiding social media and other distractions during work hours.

Practice mindfulness: Mindfulness is the practice of being present in the moment and fully engaged in the task at hand. By practicing mindfulness, we can reduce stress and improve our focus and productivity. Mindfulness can be practiced through activities such as meditation, yoga, or simply taking a few deep breaths before beginning a task.

Create a support system: Finding balance is much easier when we have a support system in place. This may include friends, family, coworkers, or a therapist. Having someone to talk to and lean on can help us navigate the challenges of finding balance.

Take breaks: Taking breaks throughout the day is essential for maintaining balance. Regular breaks can help us recharge and reduce stress. It's important to take short breaks throughout the day, as well as longer breaks such as vacations or weekends away.

Set realistic goals: Setting realistic goals is essential for finding balance. It's important to set goals that are achievable and aligned with our values and priorities. This can help us avoid burnout and maintain a sense of purpose and fulfillment.

The Benefits of Balance

When we find balance between work and life, we experience a wide range of benefits. Here are some of the benefits of balance:

Improved physical health: Finding balance can help us reduce stress, which can have a positive impact on our physical health. It can also help us prioritize self-care activities such as exercise and healthy eating, which can improve our overall well-being.

Enhanced mental health: Finding balance can also have a positive impact on our mental health. It can help us reduce stress and improve our ability to focus and think clearly.

Increased productivity: When we find balance, we're better able to manage our time and energy, which can lead to increased productivity both at work and in our personal lives.

Stronger relationships: When we prioritize our personal lives, we're able to nurture our relationships with loved ones, which can strengthen our connections and enhance our overall happiness.

Greater sense of purpose: When we find balance between work and life, we're better able to align our actions with our values and priorities. This can give us a greater sense of purpose and fulfillment in all areas of our lives.

Finding balance between work and life is essential for our well-being and happiness. By setting clear boundaries, prioritizing self-care, using technology wisely, practicing mindfulness, creating a support system, taking breaks, and setting realistic goals, we can achieve a sense of harmony and flow in our lives.

Remember, finding balance is an ongoing process, and it's important to make adjustments as needed to maintain a sense of equilibrium. By prioritizing balance in our lives, we can improve our physical, mental, and emotional health, enhance our productivity, strengthen our relationships, and cultivate a greater sense of purpose and fulfillment.

Chapter 34: Cultivating Balance in Mind, Body, and Spirit

In today's world, it can be easy to become lost in the chaos and noise of our daily lives. We may feel like we're constantly running on autopilot, moving from one task to the next without pausing to take a breath. As a result, we may find ourselves feeling disconnected from our bodies, minds, and spirits.

However, by cultivating balance in mind, body, and spirit, we can begin to find a sense of grounding and connection that allows us to navigate life's challenges with greater ease and resilience.

In this chapter, we'll explore what it means to cultivate balance in mind, body, and spirit, and offer some practical tips for doing so.

What is Balance?

Balance is the state of equilibrium and harmony between different aspects of our lives. When we are in balance, we feel a sense of peace and contentment, and are able to navigate life's challenges with greater ease and grace.

In order to cultivate balance, we must attend to all aspects of ourselves - mind, body, and spirit - and ensure that they are all nourished and cared for.

Cultivating Balance in the Mind

Our minds are powerful tools that can either work for us or against us. When our minds are balanced and clear, we are able to think more clearly and make better decisions. However, when our minds are cluttered and overwhelmed, we may feel anxious and stressed.

Here are some tips for cultivating balance in the mind:

Practice mindfulness: Mindfulness is the practice of being present in the moment and fully engaged in the task at hand. By practicing mindfulness, we can reduce stress and improve our focus and productivity. Mindfulness can be practiced through activities such as meditation, yoga, or simply taking a few deep breaths before beginning a task.

Engage in creative activities: Engaging in creative activities such as writing, painting, or playing music can help us quiet our minds and find a sense of flow and ease. These activities allow us to tap into our inner wisdom and creativity, and can help us find new perspectives on life's challenges.

Limit screen time: Spending too much time on our devices can lead to overwhelm and stress. It's important to set boundaries around our screen time and limit our exposure to social media and other digital distractions.

Cultivating Balance in the Body

Our bodies are the vessels through which we experience life. When our bodies are balanced and healthy, we are able to move through the world with greater ease and vitality. However, when our bodies are neglected or overworked, we may experience physical discomfort and pain.

Here are some tips for cultivating balance in the body:

Eat a healthy diet: Eating a diet that is rich in whole foods such as fruits, vegetables, and lean proteins can help us maintain optimal health and energy levels. It's important to listen to our bodies and pay attention to how different foods make us feel.

Engage in regular exercise: Regular exercise can help us maintain physical health and reduce stress. It's important to find an exercise routine that works for our individual needs and preferences.

Get enough sleep: Sleep is essential for physical health and mental well-being. It's important to prioritize sleep and establish a consistent sleep routine.

Cultivating Balance in the Spirit

Our spirits are the core of our being, and when we cultivate balance in our spirits, we are able to connect with a deeper sense of purpose and meaning. This can help us navigate life's challenges with greater grace and resilience.

Here are some tips for cultivating balance in the spirit:

Practice gratitude: Practicing gratitude can help us cultivate a sense of abundance and contentment. By focusing on the things we are grateful for, we are able to shift our perspective and find joy in the present moment.

Connect with nature: Spending time in nature can help us connect with a sense of awe and wonder, and remind us of our connection to something greater than ourselves. Whether it's going for a hike, taking a walk in the park, or simply sitting outside and observing the world around us, spending time in nature can help us feel more grounded and centered.

Engage in spiritual practices: Engaging in spiritual practices such as meditation, prayer, or ritual can help us connect with our inner selves and a higher power. These practices can help us cultivate a sense of peace and purpose, and provide us with guidance and support in navigating life's challenges.

Find community: Connecting with others who share our values and beliefs can help us feel supported and connected. Whether it's joining a spiritual community or simply spending time with friends and family, cultivating strong relationships can help us feel more connected to ourselves and the world around us.

Cultivating balance in mind, body, and spirit is an ongoing process that requires intention and attention. By taking care of all aspects of ourselves, we can find a sense of grounding and connection that allows us to navigate life's challenges with greater ease and resilience.

Whether it's through mindfulness practices, regular exercise, or connecting with nature, there are many ways we can cultivate balance in our lives. By making these practices a part of our daily routine, we can create a foundation of health and well-being that will serve us well throughout our lives.

Chapter 35: Living a Mindful and Balanced Life

Living a mindful and balanced life is a journey, not a destination. It requires us to be present, aware, and intentional in our thoughts and actions. It also requires us to cultivate balance in all aspects of our lives - mind, body, and spirit. In this chapter, we'll explore what it means to live a mindful and balanced life, and offer some practical tips for doing so.

What is Mindfulness?

Mindfulness is the practice of being fully present and engaged in the present moment, without judgment or distraction. It involves paying attention to our thoughts, feelings, and sensations with curiosity and openness, rather than trying to push them away or ignore them.

Mindfulness can help us reduce stress, improve our focus and productivity, and cultivate a sense of inner peace and well-being. It can also help us develop greater self-awareness, empathy, and compassion for others.

Here are some tips for cultivating mindfulness in your daily life:

Start your day with intention: Set aside a few minutes each morning to set your intentions for the day. Take a few deep breaths and focus on what you want to accomplish or how you want to show up in the world. This can help you start your day with a sense of purpose and direction.

Practice mindful breathing: Whenever you feel stressed or overwhelmed, take a few deep breaths and focus on your breath. Notice the sensation of air entering and leaving your body, and allow your mind to quiet and settle.

Tune into your senses: Take a few moments each day to tune into your senses - notice the sights, sounds, smells, and sensations around you. This can help you cultivate a greater sense of presence and awareness.

Take mindful breaks: Throughout the day, take short breaks to check in with yourself and reset your energy. This could involve taking a short walk outside, doing a quick meditation or yoga practice, or simply taking a few deep breaths.

Cultivating Balance in Mind, Body, and Spirit

Living a mindful and balanced life also involves cultivating balance in all aspects of our lives - mind, body, and spirit. When we attend to all of these areas of our lives, we can experience greater health, happiness, and well-being.

Here are some tips for cultivating balance in mind, body, and spirit:

Nourish your mind: Engage in activities that nourish your mind, such as reading, writing, or learning new skills. Avoid overstimulation from social media and other digital distractions, and practice mindfulness to help quiet and calm your mind.

Care for your body: Eat a healthy diet, engage in regular exercise, and prioritize sleep to help keep your body in balance. Listen to your body and give it the rest and recovery it needs.

Connect with your spirit: Practice gratitude, spend time in nature, and engage in spiritual practices such as meditation, prayer, or journaling to connect with your inner self and cultivate a deeper sense of purpose and meaning.

Set boundaries: Establish clear boundaries around your time, energy, and relationships to help protect your well-being and maintain balance in your life. This may involve saying no to certain commitments, limiting your exposure to toxic people or environments, and prioritizing self-care.

Bringing Mindfulness and Balance into Your Daily Life

Living a mindful and balanced life requires us to be intentional and proactive in our approach to life. Here are some practical tips for bringing mindfulness and balance into your daily life:

Create a routine: Establish a consistent routine that includes time for self-care, work, play, and rest. This can help you stay grounded and centered, even in the midst of a busy or chaotic schedule.

Practice gratitude: Take time each day to reflect on the things you are grateful for. This can help shift your focus from what is lacking in your life to what you already have, and cultivate a greater sense of joy and contentment.

Engage in mindful communication: Practice active listening and speak with intention and clarity when communicating with others. This can help you build deeper connections and avoid misunderstandings or conflicts.

Embrace imperfection: Recognize that living a mindful and balanced life is a journey, and that it's okay to make mistakes or have setbacks along the way. Embrace the process of growth and learning, and be kind and gentle with yourself.

Practice self-compassion: Treat yourself with the same kindness and compassion that you would offer to a close friend or loved one. This can help you build resilience and bounce back from difficult situations.

Take time for reflection: Set aside time each day or week to reflect on your thoughts, emotions, and experiences. This can help you gain greater insight into yourself and your life, and make adjustments as needed.

Living a mindful and balanced life is not always easy, but it is always worth the effort. By cultivating mindfulness and balance in our lives, we can experience greater health, happiness, and well-being, and live with greater purpose and meaning.

Remember, mindfulness and balance are not destinations to be reached, but rather ongoing practices to be cultivated. By incorporating these practices into your daily life, you can create a more intentional, fulfilling, and joyful life for yourself and those around you. So take the first step today, and begin your journey towards a more mindful and balanced life.

Part 9:
The Power Within

Chapter 36: The Power Within You

Deep within each of us lies a power that is often untapped, unrecognized, and underutilized. This power is our inner strength, our inner light, and our inner voice. It is the essence of who we are, and it is waiting to be unleashed.

In this chapter, we will explore the power within you, and offer some practical tips for tapping into it and harnessing it to live your best life.

The Power Within You

The power within you is your inner strength, your inner light, and your inner voice. It is the source of your creativity, your inspiration, and your motivation. It is the essence of who you are, and it is waiting to be unleashed.

The power within you is not something that you can buy or acquire. It is not something that you can learn from a book or a seminar. It is not something that you can get from someone else. It is something that you already have, and it is waiting to be discovered.

Tapping into the Power Within You

Tapping into the power within you requires you to do three things: believe in yourself, listen to your inner voice, and take action.

Believe in yourself: Believing in yourself means having faith in your abilities, your talents, and your worth. It means knowing that you are capable of achieving great things, and that you are worthy of love and respect. It also means recognizing that you have flaws and weaknesses, and accepting them as part of who you are.

Listen to your inner voice: Your inner voice is your intuition, your gut feeling, and your inner wisdom. It is the voice that tells you what you really want, what is important to you, and what is true for you. It is the voice that guides you towards your purpose and your passion. To listen to your inner voice, you need to quiet your mind, tune in to your body, and pay attention to your feelings.

Take action: Taking action means stepping out of your comfort zone, facing your fears, and doing what you need to do to achieve your goals. It means taking small steps towards your dreams, even if you don't know exactly where they will lead you. It means being willing to make mistakes, learn from them, and keep moving forward.

Practical Tips for Tapping into the Power Within You

Here are some practical tips for tapping into the power within you:

Meditate: Meditation is a powerful tool for quieting your mind, tuning in to your body, and connecting with your inner voice. Try setting aside a few minutes each day to sit in silence, breathe deeply, and focus on your inner world.

Journal: Writing in a journal is a great way to connect with your inner voice, explore your thoughts and feelings, and gain clarity on what you want and need in life. Try writing in your journal each morning or evening, and see what insights and inspiration emerge.

Visualize: Visualization is a powerful technique for tapping into your inner power and manifesting your dreams. Close your eyes, and imagine yourself achieving your goals, living your ideal life, and feeling fulfilled and happy.

Practice self-care: Taking care of yourself is essential for tapping into your inner power. Make sure you are getting enough sleep, eating a healthy diet, and engaging in activities that bring you joy and relaxation.

Surround yourself with positive people: The people you surround yourself with can have a big impact on your ability to tap into your inner power. Surround yourself with people who uplift and support you, and avoid those who bring you down or drain your energy.

The power within you is a force to be reckoned with. It is the source of your creativity, your inspiration, and your motivation. It is the essence of who you are, and it is waiting to be unleashed. By believing in yourself, listening to your inner voice, and taking action, you can tap into this power and live your best life.

Remember, the power within you is not something that can be bought or acquired. It is something that already exists within you, waiting to be discovered and utilized. By following the practical tips outlined in this chapter, you can begin to access this power and unleash your true potential.

Believe in yourself, listen to your inner voice, and take action. These three simple steps can help you tap into the power within you and live a more fulfilling and meaningful life. So go ahead, take that first step, and see where your inner power can take you. The possibilities are endless.

Chapter 37: Connecting with Your Inner Power

Connecting with your inner power is about tapping into the vast potential that lies within you. It is about unlocking the energy, creativity, and inspiration that can help you achieve your goals, fulfill your purpose, and live your best life. In this chapter, we will explore what it means to connect with your inner power, and offer some practical tips for doing so.

What is Inner Power?

Inner power is the energy that resides within each of us. It is the essence of our being, and it is what gives us the strength, courage, and resilience to face life's challenges. Inner power is not something that we acquire or learn; it is something that we already have, but often fail to recognize or tap into.

Connecting with your inner power means accessing this energy and using it to create positive change in your life. It means trusting your intuition, following your heart, and embracing your authenticity. When you connect with your inner power, you tap into a source of wisdom, creativity, and inspiration that can guide you towards your purpose and help you overcome obstacles.

How to Connect with Your Inner Power

Connecting with your inner power requires a combination of self-awareness, intention, and action. Here are some practical tips for connecting with your inner power:

Get quiet

The first step to connecting with your inner power is to get quiet. This means creating a space of stillness and silence where you can tune out external distractions and turn inward. You can do this through meditation, deep breathing, or simply sitting in nature.

Listen to your intuition

Your intuition is the voice of your inner power. It is the gut feeling, the hunch, or the instinct that guides you towards what is true and right for you. To connect with your inner power, you need to listen to your intuition and trust it. This means learning to distinguish your intuition from your fears, doubts, or limiting beliefs.

Cultivate self-awareness

Self-awareness is the foundation of connecting with your inner power. It means becoming conscious of your thoughts, emotions, and behaviors, and understanding how they influence your life. You can cultivate self-awareness through practices such as journaling, self-reflection, or therapy.

Embrace your authenticity

Your inner power is most accessible when you are true to yourself. This means embracing your strengths, weaknesses, quirks, and uniqueness. It means letting go of the need to conform to others' expectations or standards, and embracing your own values and passions.

Take action

Connecting with your inner power also requires taking action. This means stepping out of your comfort zone, taking risks, and pursuing your goals. It means using your inner power to create positive change in your life and the world around you.

Practical Tips for Connecting with Your Inner Power

Here are some practical tips for connecting with your inner power:

Practice mindfulness

Mindfulness is a powerful tool for connecting with your inner power. It involves being fully present in the moment and observing your thoughts and emotions without judgment. You can practice mindfulness through meditation, yoga, or simply paying attention to your breath.

Find your flow

Your flow is the state of being where you feel fully engaged, energized, and inspired. It is where your skills and passions intersect, and where time seems to fly by. To connect with your inner power, find activities that put you in your flow, whether it's writing, painting, dancing, or gardening.

Connect with nature

Nature is a powerful source of inner power. Spending time in nature can help you tune into your senses, connect with your intuition, and feel a sense of awe and wonder. Whether it's hiking, camping, or simply taking a walk in the park, make time to connect with nature regularly.

Practice gratitude

Gratitude is a powerful practice that can help you connect with your inner power by cultivating a positive mindset and focusing on what you have rather than what you lack. Take time each day to reflect on what you are grateful for, whether it's your health, your relationships, your work, or simply the beauty of the world around you.

Surround yourself with positivity

The people and environments we surround ourselves with can have a significant impact on our energy and mood. To connect with your inner power, surround yourself with positivity and people who support and inspire you. This may mean spending less time with negative people or environments and seeking out those that uplift and encourage you.

Engage in self-care

Self-care is an important part of connecting with your inner power. It means taking care of your physical, emotional, and spiritual well-being. This may include activities such as getting enough sleep, eating healthy food, exercising regularly, and engaging in activities that bring you joy and relaxation.

Release limiting beliefs

Limiting beliefs are beliefs that hold us back from reaching our full potential. They are often formed from past experiences or external influences and can be challenging to overcome. However, by identifying and releasing limiting beliefs, you can tap into your inner power and create positive change in your life.

Connecting with your inner power is a journey of self-discovery and personal growth. It requires self-awareness, intention, and action. By tapping into the energy, creativity, and inspiration within you, you can overcome obstacles, achieve your goals, and live your best life. By following the practical tips outlined in this chapter, you can start connecting with your inner power today. Remember, your inner power is already within you; you just need to learn how to access it. Trust yourself, believe in yourself, and embrace your authenticity, and you will unlock the infinite potential that lies within you.

Chapter 38: Cultivating Your Inner Strength

Life is full of challenges and obstacles that can test our limits and push us to our breaking point. In times of struggle and adversity, it's essential to cultivate our inner strength. Inner strength is the ability to persevere through difficult times, stay centered in the face of chaos, and maintain a positive outlook despite the circumstances.

In this chapter, we will explore what it means to cultivate inner strength, and offer some practical tips for doing so.

What is Inner Strength?

Inner strength is the power that resides within each of us. It's the resilience, courage, and determination that we tap into when facing adversity. Inner strength is not something that we acquire or learn; it's something that we already have, but often fail to recognize or use.

Cultivating inner strength means accessing this power and using it to navigate life's challenges. It means trusting your inner guidance, staying grounded in your values, and maintaining a positive outlook despite the circumstances.

How to Cultivate Inner Strength:

Cultivating inner strength requires a combination of mindset, habits, and practices. Here are some practical tips for cultivating inner strength:

Cultivate a Growth Mindset:

A growth mindset is the belief that we can improve our abilities through effort and practice. When we have a growth mindset, we view failure as an opportunity for learning and growth, rather than as a personal shortcoming. Cultivating a growth mindset helps us to be more resilient and persistent when facing challenges.

Practice Self-Care:

Self-care is the practice of taking care of our physical, emotional, and mental well-being. When we prioritize self-care, we have more energy, clarity, and resilience to navigate life's challenges. Some self-care practices include getting enough sleep, eating a healthy diet, exercising regularly, and taking time for relaxation and leisure activities.

Set Boundaries:

Setting boundaries means knowing and communicating our limits and needs. When we set boundaries, we protect our energy, time, and resources from being drained by others. Setting boundaries helps us to stay centered and focused on our priorities, which strengthens our inner resolve and determination.

Practice Mindfulness:

Mindfulness is the practice of being fully present in the moment and observing our thoughts, emotions, and sensations without judgment. When we practice mindfulness, we cultivate awareness and clarity, which helps us to make better decisions and respond more effectively to challenges.

Develop Resilience:

Resilience is the ability to bounce back from setbacks and challenges. Developing resilience requires learning from our mistakes, staying focused on our goals, and maintaining a positive outlook despite the circumstances. Resilience helps us to stay motivated and persistent in the face of adversity.

Seek Support:

Seeking support means reaching out to others for help and guidance when we need it. When we seek support, we tap into the collective wisdom and strength of our community, which can help us to overcome challenges and achieve our goals. Seeking support also helps us to build trust, connection, and resilience.

Practice Gratitude:

Gratitude is the practice of acknowledging and appreciating the good things in our life. When we practice gratitude, we cultivate a positive mindset and focus on the blessings and opportunities in our life, rather than on our problems and difficulties. Gratitude helps us to stay motivated, optimistic, and resilient in the face of adversity.

Cultivating inner strength is a lifelong process that requires ongoing effort and commitment. By practicing the tips and strategies outlined in this chapter, you can develop the resilience, courage, and determination to face life's challenges with grace and confidence.

Remember, inner strength is not something that we acquire or learn; it's something that we already have, but often fail to recognize or use. By tapping into our inner strength and cultivating a growth mindset, practicing self-care, setting boundaries, practicing mindfulness, developing resilience, seeking support, and practicing gratitude, we can unleash our inner power and live our lives with purpose and passion.

Life will continue to throw challenges and obstacles our way, but with inner strength, we can face them head-on and emerge stronger and more resilient than ever before. So, let's embrace our inner strength and cultivate it every day, knowing that we have the power within us to create the life we truly desire.

Chapter 39: Living Your Best Life with the Power Within

Living your best life is about harnessing the power within you to create the life that you want. It's about aligning your thoughts, feelings, and actions with your true purpose and values, and living in a state of joy, abundance, and fulfillment.

In this chapter, we will explore how to tap into the power within you and live your best life.

What is the Power Within?

The power within is the inner wisdom, strength, and creativity that reside within each of us. It's the source of our inspiration, intuition, and imagination, and the key to unlocking our full potential.

The power within is not something that we acquire or learn; it's something that we already have, but often fail to recognize or use. It's the part of us that knows what we really want and what we're capable of achieving, and that guides us toward our true purpose and destiny.

How to Tap into the Power Within:

Tapping into the power within requires a combination of mindset, habits, and practices. Here are some practical tips for tapping into the power within and living your best life:

Connect with Your Inner Self:

Connecting with your inner self means taking time to listen to your thoughts, feelings, and intuition. It means getting quiet and still, and tuning in to the wisdom and guidance that reside within you. Some ways to connect with your inner self include meditation, journaling, and spending time in nature.

Define Your Purpose and Values:

Defining your purpose and values means identifying what's most important to you and what gives your life meaning and significance. It means aligning your goals and actions with your true purpose and values, and living in a way that's consistent with your deepest desires and aspirations.

Create a Vision:

Creating a vision means imagining the life that you want to live, and visualizing it in vivid detail. It means using your imagination and creativity to create a compelling picture of your ideal life, and using that vision as a guide for your actions and decisions.

Take Action:

Taking action means moving forward toward your goals and dreams, and taking steps to make them a reality. It means using your power and resources to create the life that you want, and taking responsibility for your own happiness and fulfillment.

Practice Gratitude:

Practicing gratitude means acknowledging and appreciating the good things in your life, and focusing on the blessings and opportunities rather than on your problems and difficulties. It means cultivating a positive mindset and attitude, and recognizing the abundance and richness of your life.

Trust Your Inner Guidance:

Trusting your inner guidance means following your intuition and inner wisdom, and allowing them to guide you toward your true purpose and destiny. It means listening to your inner voice and trusting that it knows what's best for you, even if it's not what others might expect or approve of.

Living your best life is about tapping into the power within you and aligning your thoughts, feelings, and actions with your true purpose and values. It's about creating a vision for your life, taking action to make it a reality, and trusting your inner guidance to guide you toward your destiny.

Remember, the power within is not something that we acquire or learn; it's something that we already have, but often fail to recognize or use. By connecting with your inner self, defining your purpose and values, creating a vision, taking action, practicing gratitude, and trusting your inner guidance, you can tap into the power within you and live your best life.

Chapter 40: The Power of Self-Healing with Energy

Our bodies are more than just physical vessels that require maintenance and care. They are also energetic systems that are deeply interconnected with our emotions, thoughts, and beliefs. This connection between our physical bodies and our energetic selves is the basis of energy healing.

In this final chapter, we will explore the power of self-healing with energy, and offer some practical tips for harnessing this power to live a healthier, happier life.

What is Energy Healing?

Energy healing is a holistic approach to healing that works with the energetic systems of the body to promote balance and harmony. Energy healing acknowledges that our physical bodies are influenced by our emotions, thoughts, and beliefs, and seeks to restore balance and harmony to all aspects of our being.

There are many different types of energy healing, including Reiki, Qi Gong, Acupuncture, and Chakra Healing, to name a few. Each of these modalities works with the body's energy systems in different ways to promote healing and wellbeing.

The Power of Self-Healing with Energy

While working with a trained energy healer can be a powerful and transformative experience, self-healing with energy is also a powerful tool that anyone can learn to use. By tapping into the power of our own energetic systems, we can promote healing, reduce stress, and increase our overall wellbeing.

Here are some practical tips for harnessing the power of self-healing with energy:

Practice Mindfulness:

Mindfulness is the practice of being fully present in the moment and observing our thoughts, emotions, and sensations without judgment. When we practice mindfulness, we cultivate awareness and clarity, which helps us to make better decisions and respond more effectively to challenges.

Mindfulness can also help us to connect with our own energetic systems and notice when there is an imbalance or blockage that needs to be addressed. By practicing mindfulness regularly, we can become more attuned to our own energetic needs and take proactive steps to promote healing.

Visualize Healing Energy:

Visualization is a powerful tool for tapping into the energy of healing. By visualizing healing energy flowing into your body and surrounding you, you can activate your own energetic systems and promote healing.

To practice visualization, find a quiet space where you can relax and close your eyes. Take several deep breaths to center yourself, and then visualize a bright, healing light surrounding you. Imagine this light flowing into your body, filling you with warmth, vitality, and wellbeing. Hold this visualization for several minutes, and then release it with gratitude.

Practice Energy Exercises:

There are many energy exercises that you can practice to promote healing and balance in your energetic systems. These exercises may include gentle movements, breathing exercises, or meditations that are designed to activate and balance specific energy centers in the body.

Some examples of energy exercises include Qi Gong, Tai Chi, Yoga, and Reiki. These practices can help to promote relaxation, reduce stress, and balance the energy flow in the body.

Use Crystals:

Crystals are powerful tools for harnessing the energy of healing. Each crystal has its own unique energy and properties that can be used to promote healing and balance in the body.

To use crystals for self-healing, choose a crystal that resonates with your intentions for healing. Hold the crystal in your hand, and focus your intention on the healing properties of the crystal. You can also place the crystal on the corresponding energy center in your body, such as the heart center for emotional healing or the crown center for spiritual healing.

The power of self-healing with energy is a profound and transformative tool that anyone can learn to use. By tapping into our own energetic systems and promoting balance and harmony, we can promote healing, reduce stress, and increase our overall wellbeing.

Remember, self-healing with energy is not a substitute for medical care, but it can be used in conjunction with traditional medical treatments to support healing and wellbeing.

As you continue on your journey of self-discovery and healing, remember to be patient and kind with yourself. Healing is a process that takes time and effort, but with consistent practice and dedication, you can tap into the power of your own energetic systems and live a more vibrant, fulfilling life.

Thank you for joining me on this journey through The Power Within: A Guide to Self-Healing with Energy. I hope that this book has been a valuable resource for you, and that you feel empowered to take control of your own healing journey.

Remember, the power to heal is within you. All you need to do is tap into it and let it guide you on your path to wellness and happiness.

Don't miss out!

Visit the website below and you can sign up to receive emails whenever SERGIO RIJO publishes a new book. There's no charge and no obligation.

https://books2read.com/r/B-A-COYW-WAPIC

BOOKS 2 READ

Connecting independent readers to independent writers.

Did you love *The Power Within: A Guide to Self-Healing with Energy*? Then you should read *Akashic Records and Past Lives: Understanding How Past Lives Can Impact Your Present and Future*[1] by SERGIO RIJO!

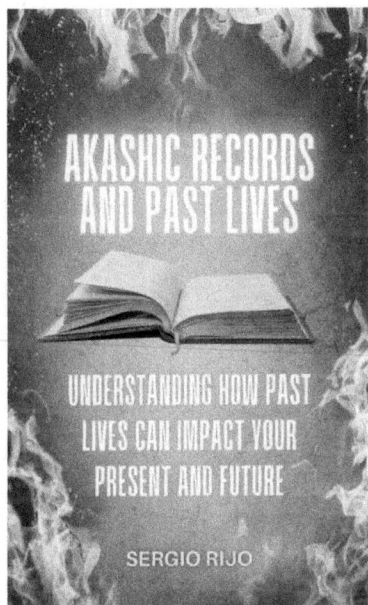

Discover the power of your past lives and unlock the secrets of the Akashic Records with this comprehensive guide. Akashic Records and Past Lives offers a step-by-step approach to accessing the Akashic Records and exploring your past lives. With clear guidance and practical tools, this book provides readers with the tools they need to understand how their past lives can impact their present and future.

Through exploring their past lives, readers will gain a deeper understanding of their soul's journey and the lessons they are meant to learn in this lifetime. The book also offers guidance on how to integrate

---

1. https://books2read.com/u/bznPvG

2. https://books2read.com/u/bznPvG

past life exploration into a spiritual practice, including meditation and energy work.

Akashic Records and Past Lives is a must-read for anyone seeking spiritual growth and personal transformation. Whether you are new to the Akashic Records or have been exploring past lives for years, this book provides valuable insights and practical tools for continued exploration. This book will inspire and empower readers to unlock their full potential and live their best lives.

Also by SERGIO RIJO

Breaking Free: A Guide to Recovery from Narcissistic Abuse
Dreamweaving: The Ultimate Guide to Entering Someone's Dreams
From Isolation to Balance: The Ultimate Guide to Remote Work Success
The Twin Flames Blueprint: A Guide to Achieving Union and Embracing the Journey
Insta-Profit: 25 Proven Ways to Monetize Your Instagram Presence
The Awakening: Archangel Michael's Message for a Unified and Evolved Humanity
Unlock Your Potential: 10 Key Skills for Young People to Have Success in Life and Career
30 Days of Spiritual Transformation: How to Change Your Life Through the Power of Spirituality
Brain Overhaul: Upgrading Your Mind for Accelerated Learning and Success
30 Days to a Richer You: The Millionaire Success Habits That Will Change Your Life
Separate but Connected: A Guide to Navigating the Twin Flame Separation Stage
The Rise of AI Income: Using Artificial Intelligence for Financial Success
Anime Tattoo Design Book: 300+ Designs for Fans and Tattoo Artists
The Art of Butterfly Tattoos: 300+ Designs to Inspire Your Next Tattoo

Rose Tattoo Designs: 300+ Designs to Inspire Your Next Tattoo

The Geometric Tattoo Handbook: A Complete Collection of 300+ Designs

Skull Tatoo Designs: Over 300 Tattoo Designs to Inspire You

Soulful: Unlocking the 16 Traits of Advanced Souls

Memory Mastery: The Proven System to Retain Information Effectively

Rise and Shine: A Guide to Kundalini Awakening for the Modern Spiritual Seeker

The Power of Presence: Connecting with Your Higher Self and Living with Purpose

Powerful Techniques for Mastering the Art of Influence: Proven Strategies to Exert Maximum Power and Persuasion

The Art of Remote Viewing: A Step-by-Step Guide to Unlocking Your Psychic Abilities

Money Magnetism: The Art of Attracting Abundance

The Happiness Handbook: A Practical Guide to Finding Joy and Fulfillment

The Smarter You: Proven Ways to Boost Your Intelligence

Appetite Control Strategies: The Secret to Successful Weight Loss

Off The Grid Living: A Comprehensive Guide to Sustainable and Self-Sufficient Living

The Ultimate Guide to Get Your Ex Back: A Step-by-Step Blueprint to Rekindle Love and Heal Your Relationship

Calm and Centered: Overcoming Anxiety and Panic Attacks Naturally

The Power Within: Boosting Self-Esteem and Confidence through Positive Self-Talk and Self-Care Practices

Grateful Living: Transform Your Life with the Power of Gratitude

Procrastination Uncovered: Understanding and Overcoming the Epidemic of Delay

Social Butterfly: Tips and Strategies for Conquering Shyness and Social Anxiety

Living with Purpose: Finding Meaning and Direction in Life

Breaking Free from Self-Sabotage: Overcoming Destructive Patterns and Achieving Your Goals

Uncovering the Shadows: A Journey through Shadow Work

The Science of Nutrition for Athletes: Understanding the Specific Nutritional Needs of Athletes for Optimal Performance and Recovery

The Magic of Saying No: How to Establish Boundaries and Take Charge of Your Life

Connecting with the Divine: Tools and Techniques for Powerful Prayer

Living in Harmony: The Complete Guide to Permaculture and Sustainable Living

Angelic Assistance: How to Connect with Your Guardian Angels and Spirit Guides for Support

Beyond Belief: Unraveling the Psychology of Ghosts and Hauntings

Transform Your Health with Intermittent Fasting: A Comprehensive Guide to Techniques and Benefits

Discover the Secrets of Lucid Dreaming: How to Use Your Dreams to Transform Your Life

Existential Crisis: Strategies for Finding Hope and Renewal in Life's Darkest Moments

The 12 Spiritual Laws of the Universe: A Comprehensive Guide to Achieving Personal Growth and Spiritual Enlightenment

The 144,000 Lightworkers: Healing and Awakening Humanity to Save the World

Defying Age: The Ultimate Guide to Living a Long and Healthy Life

Unlocking the Secrets of Astral Projection: Techniques for Successful Out-of-Body Experiences

Inner Child Healing: The Key to Overcoming Negative Beliefs, Self-Sabotage, and Unlocking Your True Potential

Raising Your Vibration: A Holistic Guide to Achieving Emotional and Spiritual Well-being

The Power Within: A Guide to Self-Healing with Energy

About the Author

Join me on an adventure through captivating stories! I'm Sergio Rijo, a passionate writer with 20 years of experience in crafting books across genres. Let's explore new worlds together and get hooked from start to finish.

www.ingramcontent.com/pod-product-compliance
Lightning Source LLC
LaVergne TN
LVHW022201221224
799742LV00031B/668